SAMARKAND

A Visit to the Russians in Central Asia

A Visit to the Russians
in
Central Asia

by

Isabelle Mary Phibbs

Ross & Perry, Inc.
Washington, D.C.

© Ross & Perry, Inc. 2001 All rights reserved.

Protected under the Berne Convention. Published 2001

Printed in The United States of America

Ross & Perry, Inc. Publishers
717 Second St., N.E., Suite 200
Washington, D.C. 20002
Telephone (202) 675-8300
Facsimile (801) 459-7535
info@RossPerry.com

SAN 253-8555

Library of Congress Control Number: 2001097803
http://www.rossperry.com

ISBN 1-931839-45-X

Image on cover provided by Alan Bowker

⊗ The paper used in this publication meets the requirements for permanence established by the American National Standard for Information Sciences "Permanence of Paper for Printed Library Materials" (ANSI Z39.48-1984).

All rights reserved. No copyrighted part of this publication may be reproduced, stored in a retrieval system, or transmitted, in any form or by any means, electronic, photocopying, recording, or otherwise, without the prior written permission of the publisher.

LIST OF ILLUSTRATIONS

	PAGE
FRONTISPIECE	
PILGRIMAGE CHURCH OF ST DAVID	15
TIFLIS	19
BRIDGE OVER THE KUR, TIFLIS	33
PERSIAN CITADEL, BAKU	37
BAKU, WITH MAIDEN'S TOWER	41
NAPHTHA SPRING, BAKU	45
GÉOK TÉPÉ. INSIDE THE FORT	51
TURKOMANS, GÉOK TÉPÉ	55
STATION AT ASKABAD	59
TURKOMAN AUL	67
KOSSAKS	75
PICNIC AFTER SHAM FIGHT, MERV	91
MEDRESSÉ. TURKOMAN VILLAGE	95
TURKOMAN WOMEN MAKING CARPETS	99
OLD MERV	113
OLD MERV	131
MEDRESSÉ AND TOWER, BUCHARA	153
THE TOWER OF BUCHARA	161
PRISONERS OF BUCHARA	165

LIST OF ILLUSTRATIONS

	PAGE.
CITADEL OR ARK, BUCHARA	171
SHAH ZINDEH, SAMARKAND	181
TOMB OF TIMUR (EXTERIOR), SAMARKAND	187
TOMB OF TIMUR (INTERIOR), SAMARKAND	197
TOMB OF TIMUR—TRACING OF DESIGN ON JADE	201
TOMB OF TIMUR (EXTERIOR), SAMARKAND	205
SHAH ZINDEH, SAMARKAND	209
SACRED TOMB, SHAH ZINDEH	213
MOSQUE OF BÌBI KHANYM, SAMARKAND	217
MOSQUE OF ULUGH BEG, RIGHISTAN, SAMARKAND	221
DECORATIVE WORK, SHAH ZINDEH	225
CAMELS IN THE DESERT	233

MAP AT THE END.

A VISIT TO THE RUSSIANS IN CENTRAL ASIA

THE advance of Russia throughout the whole of Central Asia to the frontiers of Persia, Afghanistan and into the huge Chinese Empire is a matter of exceeding interest to every British subject. The number of books written by Englishmen acquainted with these distant regions is necessarily small, from the difficulty encountered in travelling through the Russian Asiatic Provinces.

We have heard much of the great Transcaspian Railway, of which the Russians are so justly proud, bringing within reach of European travellers the wonders of Samarkand, Buchara and the historic country, full of memories of Alexander the Great, of early Christian civilization, of the terrible ravages and barbaric splendour of a Chingiz Khan or a Tamerlane.

The Russians have carefully guarded from observation the progress they have made by gigantic strides in a marvellously short space of time. Travellers who have seen the immense benefits their rule has brought to Central Asia will hesitate to condemn as unnecessary their relentless severity in the past. Wild tribes, that made peace and prosperity impossible by their marauding habits, have become law-abiding subjects, still devoted to out-door pursuits, but appearing to be proud to have their children taught in excellent schools, sitting side by side in the same classes as their Russian companions. Grievous tidings from various parts of British possessions of frequent risings and disaffection among the frontier tribes, of murders and the loss of valuable lives, lead one to think that there is something to be said in favour of Russian methods even from a humanitarian point of view. Their mode of warfare and treatment of the vanquished are in accordance with the traditions of every conqueror in these countries.

Great questions of this nature may be left for the consideration of the brilliant writers who have already done so much to awaken interest in the subject and to impart information to the reading public of England. The writer of these pages has no pretension to do more than describe scenes and lands hitherto beyond the reach of ordinary travellers.

The courteous hospitality of General Kuropatkin, Governor-General of the Transcaspian Provinces of Central Asia—now Minister of War at Petersburg—enabled a small party of English ladies and gentlemen to travel by the celebrated Transcaspian Railway as far as Samarkand, received everywhere with the most gratifying attentions, and assisted at every point of the long journey by the ready tact and kindness of the officers who accompanied them. Their introduction was obtained through a Polish nobleman, a retired officer and Chevalier of the Order of St George. The journey took place in the months of November and December 1897.

British tourists, as a rule, are apt naïvely to imagine that their presence must be welcome everywhere. Provided with a passport, they can now put to the proof this fondly cherished idea. Hitherto their wanderings have not been encouraged beyond the eastern limits of the Black Sea. At the present time ladies travelling alone can, without the slightest difficulty, visit the interesting town of Tiflis, passing through part of the splendid scenery of the Caucasus. Should their curiosity tempt them so far, they can continue their journey to the hideous naphtha-sodden town of Baku. The *bad sailor* will probably prefer to travel by land through Russia, descending to Tiflis from Vladikavkas by the wonderful Pass of Dariel. But this can be done only in fine weather, as the road is liable to be blocked by the first heavy fall of snow.

Musulman tradition says that the mountains of the Caucasus are guarded by the legendary giants Gog and Magog called Jajul and Majul, and that one of the twenty-five signs of the end of the world will be the irruption of countless myriads of their followers, and their descent into the plains below. It would be interesting to know if the Russian advance is looked upon as a "sign of the times." The legend of the giants naturally takes another form in England, and I believe that it is interpreted in every country in a different manner. Of Gog and Magog, as they were called by the Hebrews, there are wonderful tales in the Arabian histories. Their descendants were believed to be the Hyperboreans of the Greeks. An old French writer, quoting from an Oriental work, says that in 842, Vathek, ninth Khalif of the Abbassides, wishing to know more of the celebrated rampart built by Alexander the Great to prevent the incursions of these wild hordes, sent his minister Salem, with a company of fifty persons, from Samara in Chaldea, his capital, to the King of Armenia at Sis. Travelling thence to Derbend, on the

Caspian Sea, he passed through the territory of the Alans, a people mentioned by Josephus who still maintain their nationality. In this chronicle mention is made of fishing in the waters of the Caspian Sea, with marvellous tales of fictitious mermaids. More interesting are the allusions to an evil-smelling land, "un pays qui sentait fort mauvais." This may well mean the horrible smell of petroleum pervading the whole country round the modern town of Baku. Near Cape Plaka in the Crimea there is an extraordinary chaos of rocks, with ruins of pre-historic times, emitting a disgusting odour; that, however, would have been a very long journey for a traveller of the ninth century. Salem, before giving an account of his mission, made a journey to Samarkand through Khorasan, after an absence of two years and four months.

The Russian Steam Navigation Company's boats between Constantinople and Batum are comfortable, and the cuisine is fairly good. The most unpleasant part of the voyage is the start from Constantinople and the landing again at that dirtiest and most depressing of cities. The sail along the Bosphorus is truly magnificent, whether seen by sunset or in bright morning light, in spite of the absence of architectural beauty in the buildings that line both European and Asiatic shores. The south coast of the Black Sea is agreeable and picturesque as seen from the steamer, but melancholy from the absence of human habitations.

A visit to Trebizond, with the memory of the recent massacre of 1300 Armenians, can hardly be said to dissipate melancholy reflections. The unhappy Armenians are disliked and distrusted by Russians almost as much as by their ferocious persecutors in Turkey. They have a reputation for quick-wittedness in business matters surpassing that of the Jews. Without having the unmistakable characteristics of the Jewish race, it is remarkable that they can be distinguished at a glance from Georgians, Kossaks, or any of the people dwelling in the country that was originally called Armenia. It is unfortunate that travellers from the West have seldom the opportunity of knowing Armenians of the "upper" or educated classes.

I visited Trebizond late in the day in unfavourable circumstances. Rain had just ceased, and the landswell which is peculiar to the place was unpleasant. The harbour, built by the Emperor Hadrian, has long ago been destroyed, and, as has been amusingly remarked, "Turkey does not interfere with nature in such things, nor in the matter of roads." Boats push off from land to meet the steamers, but climbing up from or down into them is by no means an easy process. The boats on the coast of Asia Minor are picturesque with their antique high prows suggestive of the unchanging East.

It is difficult to realize that this was the last stronghold of the Eastern Empire. Little remains of its former greatness, and it has now a general air of poverty and squalor.

There can be no doubt about the horrible massacres that have taken place here, but numbers may be exaggerated.

Trebizond, once the port for commerce with Persia *via* Erzerum, has lost its importance since Batum has monopolized the eastern trade of the Black Sea. This Russian town is being extensively enlarged and improved. It has a beautiful garden promenade on the shores of the Euxine, and a grand background of mountains. The railway station is rather far from the landing stage, but it is finely situated on high ground at the back of the town. A cordial reception was given to the English travellers, with a banquet in a hall decorated with British flags and words of welcome. The complimentary toasts, accompanied by our National Anthem and the beautiful Russian Hymn, were duly honoured.

It should not be forgotten that the Russo-Turkish treaty of Adrianople, 1829, opened the Black Sea to commerce, and in 1831 an English sailing boat began to ply between

Constantinople and Trebizond. Dr Sandwith's charming book on the Siege of Kars gives very amusing details on the subject.

At Batum there are gigantic naphtha refining stores. I was unpleasantly reminded of the fact when, whilst walking on the shingle by the sea, I picked up a few pebbles to carry home as a souvenir. I fancied that some of them were particularly attractive, with a sort of iridescent colouring. The disillusion was great when I discovered that this appearance was owing to a coating of the obnoxious oil which is always *en évidence* on the railway from Batum to the farthest point of the Transcaspian Railway. I must say that it is at Baku only that the detestable odour can be detected.

The eastern shores of the Black Sea are very unhealthy. I should not have supposed so but for the marshy jungle through which the railway passes on leaving Batum. Farther on the line threads its way through a magnificent spur of the Caucasian Mountains.

My first view of it was by night, and so completely was I fascinated by the wild beauty of the scenery that, regardless of fatigue, I stood gazing out of the windows of the corridor carriage during the whole length of the journey.

The country is full of historic interest. From the earliest ages the wild tribes of the mountains have been at war with each other, and sympathy with the desperate struggles for freedom of the warrior Schamyl, in recent times, ought not to blind us to the benefits of peace under the stern rule of the Muscovites. Looking south, one naturally thinks of one's own countrymen and the gallant deeds of "Williams of Kars" and his brave companions. The record of that memorable siege is like a page of the old chronicles of chivalry. General Murâvieff, the ideal conquering hero, generous and courteous to the officers who surrendered to him, kind and benevolent to the exhausted soldiers and starving inhabitants whom he clothed and fed. It is pleasant to dwell upon this bright exception to the harshness and duplicity which stain the record of the Russian progress.

There are many interesting places between Batum and Tiflis. From the Rion station, on the river of that name, is a short branch line to Kutais, the ancient Cyta, the farthest point of Jason's journey in search of the Golden Fleece.

Tiflis has been in the possession of Russia since 1801. It is a large town, full of sharp contrasts, combining in itself the old customs and life of the East with the latest developments of modern civilization. The English traveller will be surprised to find electric light, tramways, fine buildings, gardens, a museum, opera house, good shops, and an excellent hotel. But he will find also roads that vie with Constantinople in their disgraceful condition; in wet weather a sea of mud conceals boulders and pits in the best streets; elsewhere no attempt is made to keep a clear roadway. The native driver dashes over every obstacle at breakneck speed, regardless of the nerves or comfort of his employer. His costume is of the usual Russian type, flat cap, loosely-fitting coat with skirt of thick rounded folds that have the appearance of being stuffed with wadding. The single horses are harnessed with the high yoke, to which bells are often attached; in the case of tradesmen's vehicles they are less pleasingly adorned with the name and address of their proprietors. Coachmen driving private carriages have often dark blue braid on their coats, and folds of the same colour round their huge waists; part of the reins are also of dark blue braid, the effect is good, especially with black horses. The *troika*, with three horses abreast, is not much used at Tiflis.

The bazaars are interesting to strangers. I had not realized that a street of small shops would come under that denomination. It is startling sometimes in the smaller quarters of the town, when you are gazing at the contents of the shelves in the windows, to see a diminutive pane withdrawn and some object offered to your attention, probably the very thing that you would not admire. The silver waist-buckles, in tiny imitation of the Georgian belt and dagger, are very pretty. The word Kavkaz —Caucasus—is imprinted upon almost every object from daggers to thimbles. Furs and carpets may be bought by connoisseurs, but I can say nothing on the subject; doubting my own judgment and detesting the haggling of the bazaars, I contented myself with small purchases.

The Hôtel d'Orient is exactly opposite to a gorgeous modern church, beside which is the Royal Palace, and immediately behind them begins the ascent to wild mountains, from which may be enjoyed glorious views of the Caucasian Mountains. Kasbek, the giant, three thousand feet higher than Mont Blanc, towers over all, Mount Elbruz not being within view. The pilgrimage church of St David is a conspicuous point in most views of Tiflis. One of the most interesting "sights" is the naturally warm stream known to the Romans and used

PILGRIMAGE CHURCH OF ST DAVID

for baths; there are remains of late Roman work, *Opus Saracenesca*, and in this stream the Tiflis women work hard at washing; as usual in the East, a man who is supposed to superintend, does nothing. It is curious to see brightly coloured carpets plunged into the flowing water. The modern baths are quite "up-to-date," offering every refinement of luxury.

The "soldiers' bazaar" is held every Sunday in a small park, and the curious medley of cheap objects offered for sale is extremely amusing. I saw large sacks containing the seeds of the Pinus Strobus, commonly used for food. A more good-tempered crowd it would be impossible to find. Georgian is the language chiefly spoken.

There are two Catholic churches in Tiflis. The Polish church, always crowded with soldiers on Sunday; and the Armenian, which is also very poor.

The long ranges of mountains on each side of the valley of the Kur are very tempting to those who care for exercise in the English sense of the word. I saw something of the wide expanse of bare and somewhat dreary mountains, but a caution about brigands from official quarters restricted my wanderings.

The dress of the women of Tiflis is not pleasing. They wear across the forehead a stiff band of black velvet with a small brooch in front, which reminded me of pictures of our great-grandmothers; from it falls a white net veil, over that another veil or shawl of cashmere in black or brown, not altogether covering it, and having a very untidy appearance. The dress of the men is much more attractive; they have the monopoly of ornaments, their belts are richly adorned with silver. Silver topped rows of cartouches across the breast look handsome on the brown "kaftan" worn by Kossaks and Armenians with the high head-piece of fur. The Georgians generally wear black. The belt is in some places a mark of office.

There are many handsome private houses as well as good shops in Tiflis; cakes and bonbons

TIFLIS

will satisfy those whose taste lies in that direction, and "objets de luxe" from Paris of almost every description are to be found. The principal modern street is planted with trees like a boulevard, but it is so unnecessarily wide that crossing on foot is disagreeable in dry weather from clouds of dust, and on rainy days from the pools of water that are not easily avoided when you are endeavouring to escape from the splashes of the galloping droskies.

In the smaller shops at Tiflis I found that German was more generally understood than French; this fact is accounted for by the existence of a colony of Germans, who came originally from Wurtemburg and taught the people to cultivate the vines that produce very good light wine in the Caucasus. Game of all kinds is abundant, and we are interested to be reminded that the river Phasis gives its name to the bird (pheasant) now so familiar in Western countries.

The English travellers were hospitably entertained at luncheon by the Colonel of a Dragoon regiment stationed at a fort on the hills south of the town. The day, unfortunately, was very cold ; and the wind, which is a constant drawback to enjoyment in Tiflis, was piercing, making the surrounding mountains look dark and sombre, with much of the effect of a black east wind in England. The time, however, passed very pleasantly, the band of the dragoons played at intervals, and the songs and dances of the Kossaks, quite new to me, were extremely interesting. There was nothing in the appearance of the men to suggest the ferocity that I had always associated with their nature. They seemed to enjoy themselves and to be pleased with the evident appreciation of their talents. I cannot say much for their personal attractions. "La Cosaque," as the French call it—I do not think there is a special name for the dance in any other western nation — is difficult to describe as danced by the soldiers. Some sudden movements are by no means elegant, though they must be exceedingly difficult to execute ; the short running step, with one arm extended and the other bent with the hand at the waist or folded across the chest, requires much practice to be done with steadiness. Many of the men beat time to the music with their hands, and one is naturally led to join in this accompaniment, though probably it is not in accordance with strict etiquette. It must be encouraging to the dancers as well as the occasional shout in which a Scotch gentleman was irresistibly tempted to join, with an upward movement of the hand and arm very familiar to his countrymen. The Kossaks evidently understood the "touch of nature," and felt gratified. The usual loyal and complimentary toasts were proposed during the luncheon, and at the end the soldiers cheering their Colonel raised him three times in their arms, high above their heads. He must have been well used to such honours to be able to preserve a gay and still dignified appearance in so trying a situation.

Mr Oliphant remarked in his work upon Russia, that "the Cossacks cherish an unmitigated hatred against their conquerors; they have been insidiously deprived of almost every privilege which they once possessed. The Russians seem to consider that they are brought into the world for the express purpose of fighting their battles, and they are at the greatest pains to attribute to them a character for extraordinary bravery." There are, of course, many different races of Kossaks, and they have been cruelly transported from one part to another of the great empire, in the same manner in which so many tribes and nations have been weakened; but I saw no signs of hatred. On the contrary, it appeared to me that the Kossaks were the pets of the army, somewhat like the Bersaglieri in Italy. "Kozak" is the Russian word, with the accent upon the last syllable.

The wild songs of the Kossaks have a boyish ring in their gaiety, while in their sadness there is a broken strain of suffering as of an animal in pain. It is not like the Hungarian Zigeuner music, where you have the overwhelming contrasts of ecstatic joy and rapture with the wail of deepest mental anguish and despair.

The Russians are not tender in their dealings with the fallen, nor have they any consideration for their feelings. They have in many places taken stones from Tartar tombs to use as material for building. "Their nation was not formed in that brilliant school . . . when the word *honour* was synonymous with *truth*; and the *word of honour* had a sanctity, respected when all else might be forgotten. Russia drew her arts and sciences, her religion and politics from the debased Greek Empire, which also inspired her hatred of all that is Catholic. Religious intolerance is the spring of Russian policy."

I quote from the Marquis de Custine's impressions, written rather more than sixty years ago during the reign of Nicholas I. He attributed the unhappy condition of the country to the policy of Peter the Great and Catherine II., who forced modern ideas of civilization upon a people wholly incapable of receiving them. It is amusing to read his opinion that "Russia ought not only to stop, but to begin anew. The circumstance which renders Russia the most singular state now to be seen in the world is, that extreme barbarism favoured by the enslavement of the Church, and extreme civilization, imported from foreign lands, are there to be seen united."

This great nation, whose advance has been by leaps and bounds, has not had time to give to the softening influences of *chivalrous* sentiment. Respect for women and gentleness towards the weak and suffering have no part in the Russian creed. A new country—comparatively speaking—the history of whose growth to its actual gigantic proportions is one series of aggressive wars, can hardly be expected to give attention to such things as the rights of man and the education of the masses. The patriotism of the Russian Mujik is unreasoning devotion to the head of the State, who is also head of the Church. He is intensely loyal and devout; so long as he remains in ignorance he will be patient and long-suffering, but when he begins to think with intelligence, his reason will revolt at the frightful disregard of human life which has ever characterized the warlike policy of his rulers. History tells us that the cold-hearted empress Catherine II. sacrificed the lives of a detachment of her brave soldiers in the Crimea, so as to be able to send armies to conquer the land, under pretext of avenging their slaughter. The country cannot be said to have emerged from barbarism until the reign of Alexander II., who gave liberty to the serfs and abolished the general use of the "Knut." His murder by the contrivance of unpatriotic Nihilists has done more harm to the cause of humanity than centuries of oppression.

The Russian Church is undoubtedly the most intolerant and persecuting of all ecclesiastical denominations. Readers interested in these matters can refer to the articles on the Polish Nuns of Minsk in *Household Words* for May 1854, and in "Pictures of Christian Heroism, 1855," to see what measure of mercy is meted out to members of the Catholic Church. Mr Hare, in his "Walks in Rome," gives a graphic description of the tortures to which these heroic women were subjected. Poles, who are almost always Catholics, have scant justice shown them as to their churches and schools. Upon inquiry I found that the majority of young recruits for service in Central Asia were of Polish nationality; but beyond the Caspian Sea they are deprived of the means of practising their religion; there are no churches, and priests are not allowed to say Mass. The religious observances of the Mahometans are not interfered with.

It is exceedingly difficult for a stranger to form a clear idea of Russian life and Russian ways. A well-known author has said that "a nation cannot live without an ideal. . . ." The ideal of the poor Russian Mujik is the moral and spiritual infallibility of the Czar— "The Little Father"—who can do no wrong.

It appeared to me that there is much in common between the Mujik and the simple English countryman; respect for authority, love of the sovereign, patient endurance of suffering. But the comparison must not be pushed too far. Liberty, as we understand it, is unknown in Russia.

A recent American author, who charmingly describes the bright side of things, ventures to say that the Russian Church is "tolerant to all other creeds, and that its past is free from the stain of blood!" The kindly writer has been too ready to accept the assurances that he wished to believe.

In every Russian town or village the church is the most prominent object, and its situation generally gives it an imposing appearance. But the architecture leaves much to be desired, and the constant repetition of small bulbous domes is unpleasing. The interiors are monotonous from the rules restricting variety in decoration ; the same remark applies to the singing, which, however fine it may be, has, from the absence of instrumental accompaniment, an effect mournful and penitential.

Very hard things have been said of the unsettled state of Tiflis and of the cheapness at which life is held there. I can only describe things as I saw them. I walked alone through almost all the poor quarters of the town and never met with the slightest annoyance; any curiosity that my appearance might have excited was better concealed than it would have been in a crowd in an English country town. I was remarkably struck with the cleanly habits and good manners of the inhabitants. I know most of the countries of Europe, but not one the inhabitants of which are superior to these people in such matters.

The pleasure and interest that I felt in all around me must have been obvious. I lingered at the shop windows containing delicate silver work, I gazed at the huge swollen wine-skins the like of which I had never seen before. I wandered far to a caravanserai, where for the first time I saw camels in use. I spent hours in the Museum, vainly endeavouring to learn the characteristics and costumes of the innumerable Caucasian tribes. I saw there photographs of the ruins of Christian churches at Ani, so beautiful that I hope some day to visit that interesting town as well as Kars and Erzerum. The very name of Mount Ararat is tempting, but I believe that the expedition is difficult to accomplish from Tiflis.

A delightful day can be spent in visiting Mtskhéta, the ancient capital of Georgia; ancient indeed, as Tiflis has enjoyed that distinction since A.D. 499. The Georgians call it the oldest city in the world, and trace their history from about the fourth or fifth descendant from Noah. The country was originally called Iberia, and was first known in Western history when Pompey penetrated to the Caspian Sea. The wars of Mithridates, King of Pontus, with the Roman Republic, give interest to the adjoining country of Armenia, as well as to the vast extent of his conquests. His grandson Astabazes, King of

Armenia Major, was delivered as a prisoner with great treasures by Marc Antony to the cruel and rapacious Cleopatra, B.C. 34. The Armenians claim their descent from Amur the son of Shem. They were converted to Christianity by St Gregory under Pope Sylvester I., A.D. 319, about the same time as the conversion of the Emperor Constantine.

The Kings of Georgia were believed to be descended from Solomon and the Queen of Sheba—a claim which is also made for the Kings of Abyssinia. Apart from such mythical genealogies, the Bagratides are admitted to be the oldest line of Kings in the world. The last Czar of Georgia, unable to defend himself against the Persians, surrendered his country to Russia 1799, and died the following year. This was George XII., who, with so many of his ancestors, was buried at Mtskhéta. A member of the family of the Bagratides was killed at Borodino, fighting against the French under Alexander I.

The Russians have done much for Tiflis.

BRIDGE OVER THE KUR, TIFLIS

On the north side of a fine bridge over the Kur is a statue of Prince Woronzoff, who built it when Governor of the Caucasus. An extensive view of the town is to be obtained from the old castle and botanical garden. Some English gentlemen walking there, accidentally met the Persian Ambassador, who was special envoy to England for the Queen's Jubilee. He invited them to tea, and the Consul-General accepted an invitation to dine at the Hôtel d'Orient with the English travellers. He was particularly pleasant and courteous in manner, and was a type of Persian refinement and good looks. The dinner lasted a long time, and it must have been a relief to him when the tedium was broken by music and the songs of the Kossaks. He was placed in the trying position of being almost debarred from conversation, one of his fair neighbours speaking no language but English, which is unknown to him. I think that few of my countrymen in these circumstances could so successfully have maintained a calm and smiling demeanour.

I left Tiflis with regret, wishing I had time and room to carry off more souvenirs. I brought home a few gourds, made into jugs or vases of good shape and carved in outline designs. I bought a specimen of the singular knife and fork in one, which is in use among the country people.

The line which leaves Tiflis for the East is not interesting, but I shall never forget the beautiful colours of the sunset reflected over the distant mountains of Daghestan. At every station I saw a wooden erection, a sort of open tower, like the *Känsli* in Switzerland, placed where there is a special point of view. I was told that these were the sleeping places of the railway employés, where the wind brought them relief from the attacks of mosquitoes in summer.

Baku has been so minutely described that it would be wearisome to dwell upon its hideous and malodorous atmosphere. The quays might

PERSIAN CITADEL, BAKU

offer some attractions, but it is obvious that here men's minds are occupied with business, and they have no time to waste on pleasure.

I visited the market places, called bazaars and found them uninteresting, but I made my first acquaintance with a full length sturgeon, a fish which must not be mentioned to a Russian otherwise than with words of praise. I had no difficulty in expressing my appreciation of the *ikra* (caviar) which is always served before luncheon and dinner, accompanied with vodka, and *hors d'œuvres* of rather pungent flavour called "Zakuski."

There is an immense new cathedral at Baku nearly finished, in the usual style of architecture. It looks very white and imposing from its commanding situation. There will be an extensive view from its doors, but unfortunately there is nothing beautiful to see. A black cloud hangs like a pall over part of the town, and there are few remains left of the time of the Persian occupation with the exception of the massive walls of the citadel. Travellers, who know the interesting country of the Loire, will observe a singular resemblance in these walls to those of the town of Angers, which were condemned to lose the upper part of the beautiful towers, as a punishment for rebellion against the King of France in 1585.

A portion of a small and graceful mosque still remains, hidden away in a poor quarter of the town, within the walls, but it has been turned into a dwelling-house. Seen from the water the curious massive double tower near the quays has a striking effect. It is called the Maiden's Tower, from some history or legend of the fatal leap from its summit of a fair Persian bride to escape from a hated marriage.

A very unpleasant climb up a great hill on the south side of the town brings you to a cemetery which appears to have no end—a city of the dead—the ground is of heavy thick sand, you are overwhelmed with the impression that the whole world is crumbling away. It was touching to see in this far away spot a few graves with German inscriptions, "hier ruhet

BAKU, WITH MAIDEN'S TOWER

in friede." It would seem impossible to *rest in peace* near Baku.

I found the working of the naphtha springs difficult to understand; but had the guide been able to express himself clearly in French or German his explanations would have been wasted upon me, so completely was I overcome by the horrible smell of the oil. With difficulty I obtained answers to my inquiries about the great conflagration of September or October 1897. The marks of fire were still to be seen on the great sandy mountain adjoining the cemeteries. A visit to the ancient home of the fire-worshippers, called the Monastery of the Ghebers, would have been far more interesting, but unfortunately arrangements were not made for the expedition. The distance is about twelve miles. The weather was too rough for it to be possible to set on fire the oil which floats on the waters of the Caspian Sea. The effect must be wonderful on a dark night. I was greatly interested in watching the sailors and workmen about the busy port; there were types of many Eastern races, rough men, but very civil to strangers. The porters seem to carry enormous weights; they are generally bare-footed, and have from their shoulders a sort of padded stand which keeps the burden on their backs at a distance of at least a foot from the body at the waist. I lost my way among great bales of merchandise, and one of these men, guessing what ought to be my destination, with smiles and gestures guided my steps into the right path. The steamers on the Caspian are smaller than those on the Black Sea but they are sufficiently comfortable. The stewardess, an extremely obliging woman, at the moment of landing at Krasnovodsk, hurried after one of the ladies who had left her watch under her pillow, and restored the property to its grateful owner.

The servants spoke Russian only, but that was also the case at the hotel at Tiflis, where we had men only to attend to us. My very limited knowledge of the language was of great use to me, and I am encouraged to study it

NAPHTHA SPRING BAKU

more seriously and with hope of success. It is unfortunate that English people are under the impression that the difficulties in the Russian language are absolutely insurmountable, and I am afraid that those who have mastered them are not indisposed to encourage this belief.

On the morning of the 23rd of November the *Admiral Korneloff* steamed into Krasnovodsk harbour, where the English visitors were received in the name of General Kuropatkin by Colonel Brunelli, Director of the Transcaspian Line, and Monsieur de Klemm, Diplomatic Agent.

The passage from Baku was moderately fine, but the water was dark and looked gloomy. I heard the remark that Krasnovodsk was not unlike Aden. I thought the sharp outline of the rocky hills, seen from the land, very beautiful. There are here great works for the distillation of water, an important matter, as throughout Central Asia it is dangerous, even for external purposes, to make use of water that has not been boiled. At every station, or rather at every place where we remained for a short time, I observed the servants who were attached to our train, taking in supplies from the great waggons labelled " vada " water.

The train, which was to be a substitute for hotels during about three weeks, was composed of a great number of corridor carriages, each double compartment occupied by two or three persons. It was not exactly luxury, but it would have been sufficiently comfortable but for the loss of the sheets which were to have been supplied for the journey.

At first sight the idea of making a little spring from one set of carriages to the other when the train was in motion, seemed formidable, but one soon became used to it, and the speed did not exceed twenty-five miles an hour. There was a charming sitting-room for ladies, a smoking-room, dining-room, and a large open car, which was chiefly used for occasions when the travellers wished to observe any particular point on the journey, or for the purpose of expressing thanks and sad farewells. The cuisine was excellent, as General Kuropatkin had very kindly sent his own servants to accompany the train.

Colonel Brunelli and Monsieur de Klemm travelled with the English wanderers, and all felt that it was to the kindness and help of these gentlemen that the pleasure and interest of the expedition were due.

The railway station at Krasnovodsk is an imposing building; but life here must be terribly dull. That seemed to be the opinion of a young officer who had had an experience of some years, but he was too good a soldier to complain; he spoke English remarkably well, and hoped some day to visit our distant isle.

Almost immediately on leaving Krasnovodsk the line enters the weary desert that has caused the destruction of so many brave and devoted soldiers. I say soldiers advisedly, for here all are soldiers, the line has been made by soldiers for military purposes. Mr Oliphant said that when travelling in Russia he could not distinguish soldiers from policemen or railway officials. It would be easy in these days for a stranger to experience the same confusion of ideas.

The Kara Kum, or black desert, stretches away in endless and most depressing monotony as far as the eye can reach to the north; it is a great relief when to the south the beautiful outline of the Persian mountains comes in sight. Kizil Arvat is the only place of importance before arriving at the celebrated Géok Tépé. At this station a body of Turkomans met the train with their chief at their head, in holiday costume. A Russian officer explained the details of the celebrated siege. Géok Tépé had been a fortress with mud walls, still about twelve feet high, though the upper part was thrown down after the victory to cover the bodies of the slain. The circumference is more than two miles, it was defended by about 20,000 Tekke Turkomans. General Scobeleff's army numbered little more than 8,000 men. It was necessary to strike a decisive blow for the

GÉOK TÉPÉ. INSIDE THE FORT

honour of the army and to destroy the power of these savage tribes—the slave hunters of the desert.

The siege has been so graphically described that it is unnecessary to say more than that on the 24th of January 1881, Scobeleff, at the head of his troops, entered the doomed fortress through the breach made by the heroic action of a young officer of the name of Meyer, who sprang a mine at the foot of the formidable ramparts and narrowly escaped with his life. The Turkomans fought with desperate courage and the carnage was frightful. "It was not a rout, but a massacre." All hope of resistance was ended, as well as all danger of future risings and bloodshed.

I felt some disinclination to visit the scene of such awful suffering, but I could not decline the invitation of a Russian officer and I left the train, book in hand, certainly with no lack of interest. My companion inquired if I was carrying with me a guide to the country, and with a feeling of regret that I had not left my author in the carriage I showed him Curzon's "Russia in Central Asia"; his reply was, "An excellent writer, you can believe all he says." I did not visit the cotton industry which is greatly encouraged; at the moment I could think only of the gloomy scene within the walls of Géok Tépé; here is absolute desolation, not the sign of a building; you walk upon a surface dusty and uneven, suggestive of sinister thoughts that are not dispelled by the occasional remains of a splinter or a shell; or, who can tell if the bone at your feet is that of an animal or of a human being, dear perhaps to someone still alive. I cannot understand the feelings of anyone who would wish to carry away a remembrance of so ghastly a spot. About four hundred yards from the memorable breach in the wall we see the touching memorial to the gallant Russian soldiers who fell at this awful crisis in the wars that have cost so many valuable lives and brought sorrow to so many far distant homes. Full of sympathy with the victors, but saddened by such feelings, I confess

TURKOMANS, GÉOK TÉPÉ

that I had not the heart to turn my Kodak upon the group of Turkomans at the station, each one of which must have lost some friend or relative in that awful massacre! I give, however, the photograph taken by the professional artist travelling with the train.

My sentiments on the subject may have been exaggerated. The Tekke Turkomans do not probably understand respect for the vanquished. Vambéry says that they are incapable of the feeling of pity for suffering, however terrible. Certainly strong nerves are required to read his descriptions of their hideous cruelty to the miserable Persians whom they carried off as slaves for the markets of Khiva and Buchara; eight hundred were found in Géok Tépé.

Askabad, the residence of the Governor-General of Russian Transcaspian Provinces, is about two hours by train beyond Géok Tépé. The general aspect of the place is not interesting, huge squares, with houses of one story only, are unspeakably dreary. My first impression was that the arrangement must be for military purposes, but the plan is not unusual in Russia in Europe. The shops were called bazaars, and I found that anything that I admired was sure to come from Tashkend or Buchara.

The schools at Askabad were very interesting. The copy-books of the children would put to shame little people of the same age in England, notwithstanding the difficulty of the language.

It was pleasant to see children of all races sitting side by side, and the musical performance was highly creditable to the masters. There were also technical schools, but the Turkomans love only outdoor life. The Botanical Garden is still in its infancy, but full of promise. Having heard much of the danger of malaria in this country, I asked the Director if the eucalyptus was of any use as a preventative, but he told me that it could not be grown on account of the dryness of the climate. He pointed out to me that this extreme dryness causes the smoke from the engine of the trains

STATION AT ASKABAD

to vanish immediately on leaving the chimney. I had noticed the fact without being able to account for it.

I had heard so much of the *kibitkas* or tents of the Turkomans that I was exceedingly anxious to enter one, and here I had the pleasure of a visit to a Turkoman settlement or *aul*, which is the name given to an encampment of not less than twenty kibitkas. These tents are made of light wood, covered with felt; the top is the shape of a dome, with an opening in the centre for air and light and to let out the smoke of the fire, which is on the ground in the middle of the tent. This large round opening can be covered with a sort of cap of felt in wet weather. There are no windows, and the inside is hung round with rugs, some of them very handsome, and showing to advantage the swords, guns, and other arms which adorn the kibitkas. Carpets are on the ground; the tent is said to be very comfortable and warm in winter. The whole thing can be taken to pieces and packed on a camel in less than three hours. The women, of course, do this work; the men consider it beneath their dignity to do anything but look after their horses.

These are the terrible Tekke Turkomans, the most savage of all the nomad tribes. Their forays extended formerly to a great distance into Persia, whence they carried off the helpless people as slaves for Khiva, Buchara, and other wealthy Khanates. So late as 1858 Sultan Murad, the great reformer, who destroyed the janissaries of Constantinople, drove the Tekke Turkomans back to Merv, but, believing their promises of reform, left them there, only to renew in a very short time their horrible trade in human lives. " In 1840, there were 700,000 slaves in Khiva, of whom 30,000 were Persians, captured and sold by the Tekke and Yomoud Turkomans. When Wolff visited Buchara in 1844, there were 200,000 slaves in the Khanate. Shah Abbas the Great in the seventeenth century defeated the Turkomans and planted 15,000 Kurdish families on the frontier to defend the feeble inhabitants of Khorasán. The Kurds, unfortunately, adopted the predatory habits of the Turcomans, although they were always at enmity with them.

The ferocious Kurds, who have lately distinguished themselves by the massacre of helpless Armenians, cannot have required much teaching from the tribes of Central Asia. Vambéry has said that "in no people is the pride of birth stronger than in the Turkomans." They are probably descended from the Parthians of Greek and Roman times. The Tekke are the most numerous. The Yomoud and Goklan tribes inhabit the fertile regions east of the Caspian Sea, and south of the Balkans and the Kopet Dagh range of mountains. They are all robbers, and the Yomouds used to kidnap the poor fishermen and sell them as slaves. Happily the advance of the Russians has put an end to the horrors of slavery; and, apart from the loss of liberty, the Turkomans cannot find them harder rulers than the tyrannical Khans of Central Asia.

The Turkomans had neither chiefs nor rulers. The old men of the tribes gave advice, but they had no authority, and did not command.

Captain Conolly described their manner of making their bread by baking it on the hearth and covering it up in wood embers. "They also prepare bread with oil or clarified butter—the cake that the widow of Sarepta was picking up sticks to dress that she might eat with her son and then die, was made of a handful of meal and a little oil in a cruise." The cakes of the Turkomans are about three or four feet in diameter and more than an inch thick.

These people pass their time in unmitigated idleness. Either they have not yet recovered from their surprise at the sight of a railway engine and train, or they can imagine no better manner of spending their days than sitting and standing about the stations watching all that is going on. It was amusing to hear the description of their astonishment at the first sight of an engine; how they approached it cautiously, thinking it must be on fire, touched it gently with their fingers, and lastly with the tips of their tongues!

The Turkomans suffer much from ophthalmia, and they often lose both eyebrows and eyelashes, which does not add to their scanty supply of good looks. Their voices and language are not unpleasant to the ear. It is curious that in Turki "Kara" is *black* and "Kar" is *snow*.

In the kibitka that I first entered, a meal was being prepared on the embers in the middle of the tent, small pieces of mutton were being cooked on a skewer like kabobs. The ewers and metal vessels in ordinary use were of good design and graceful in shape; not Etruscan, but never common or offensive, as they so often are in England or in the western parts of France. They are probably valued heirlooms, and an offer to purchase them would be considered an insult. The population does not seem to be decreasing, judging from the numbers of hardy little children running about.

Writers differ curiously upon the subject of the personal courage of the Turkomans; some maintain that they never attack unless they are almost sure of success. There is no doubt that they fought splendidly when driven to defend themselves at Géok Tépé, and they showed also a degree of chivalrous feeling that was not to be expected from them.

There appears to be no diversity of opinion as to the cowardice of the Persians, and sympathy with them is repelled when one reads of their horrid reprisals when they happened to capture their enemies. It is said that they have been guilty of crucifying, impaling, and flaying them alive. "Improvement in Khorasan is impossible," Colonel M'Gregor declared, "with the accursed Persian system of mingled tyranny and imbecility."

That the Turkomans are callous and cruel no one can deny; but neither Persians nor Russians set them a good example. The Russians have at least cleared the land from slave markets, abolished torture and the most

TURKOMAN AUL

barbarous forms of capital punishment. It is more agreeable to think of these things than to recall the terrible massacres under Generals Lomakin and Kaufmann. Severity does not always ensure submission in Oriental countries, even after long years of foreign rule. The Russians have been unpleasantly reminded of this fact by the recent insurrection in Ferghana, the spirit of discontent spreading as far as Samarkand. It is curious that the formal proclamation of a religious war will always rouse the Musulman tribes, however indifferent they may be to the outward observance of their religion.

The Turkoman women are not veiled. They are unprepossessing in appearance, and their hard lives very soon rob them of their freshness. They have the habit of standing at the door of their tents for purposes of conversation, and so as to be able to keep watch over their children playing outside. Observing these things one is forcibly reminded of the fate of the unhappy Sisera, treacherously lured to his destruction. "Come in to me, my lord, come in, fear not." A woman accustomed to nomad life would find the nail of her tent a ready weapon to her hand.

It has been said by modern travellers that a stranger asking shelter of a Turkoman may feel in perfect safety so long as he is a guest within his tent. But, while offering hospitality, his host may be mentally calculating where and in what manner he can best relieve him of his possessions so soon as he has resumed his journey! The Turkomans keep their money in large purses made of the skin of a camel's neck—hence the expression "a neckful of money."

Among the most interesting sights at Askabad are the works for irrigation, including an Artesian well of considerable depth at some distance from the town. The engineers led the way over a bare and unattractive country; the little carriages following dashed at a gallop over the most impossible obstacles; part of the drive was interesting, being the trade route with camels into Persia, we are here very near the frontier, and not far from Meshed, the city of pilgrimage. The Persians are Shiahs, and revere the memory of the gallant Ali, son-in-law of Mohammed. The Turkomans are Sonnis or Sunnis, and look up to the Sultan of Constantinople as the head of their religion, but they appear to be indifferent in such matters, beyond their hatred of the sect that differs from them.

General Kuropatkin received the English travellers with the greatest kindness and hospitality. He invited them to a grand review and sham fight on the plains which stretch from Askabad to the mountains on the southern frontier. The weather was perfect, and the sight was extremely interesting. The spectators were gathered on a slight eminence which was supposed to be a fortress. The firing of the artillery was splendid; the big guns were close to us, in our defence, and would have done great execution had the warfare been real. General Kuropatkin commanded the attacking army, and the charge of cavalry below us was irresistible; finally the infantry came up with a rush, and we were taken prisoners. The beautiful National Hymn of Russia was played, and enthusiastic cheers were given for the Czar. The General invited us to taste the soldiers' soup, himself leading the way; we were allowed to carry off the wooden spoon which they use, as a remembrance.

Luncheon was served under a large tent on high ground. There was a sheep roasted whole, and mutton served in every variety. Zakuski (*hors d'œuvres*) and vodka, *a la Russe*, of course preceded the meal. Our gallant host rose and proposed the health of our beloved Queen; the toast was received with appreciative enthusiasm; the band played "God save the Queen," and the English cheered in their own fashion.

The health of the Emperor and Empress of Russia was at once proposed in return. The speech was unfortunate, touching upon political events in the past; but as the speaker could only express himself in English his remarks were probably not understood, and all present were too much excited to pay any attention. The thrilling tones of the Russian Hymn never fail to move all hearts. Various toasts followed, and the English visitors learned to join in the national "hourra, hourra, hourra," shortly and sharply repeated three times. The Kossaks danced outside the tent and the band played. Seated near General Kuropatkin at table, I was struck by his quiet manner and the expression of combined strength and gentleness in a countenance not otherwise remarkable. I could understand all that I had been told of the devotion to him, not only of the soldiers, but also of the conquered Turkomans, and yet he was the intimate friend and companion in arms of the terrible Scobeleff, and one of the first to enter the hapless fortress of Géok Tépé. A splendid soldier, he is said, nevertheless, to be a man of peace; it is he who has done so much to improve the condition of the people, and I heard that his portrait is to be found in the kibitkas of the native tribes.

The sound of the bugle brought this gay scene to an end; in an instant every soldier was in his place, the General rode down to take up his position at the saluting point for the march past. The uniform of the Russian soldier is incompatible with English ideas of smartness and it must be oppressive in moments of great exertion. It does not, however, interfere with the fighting powers of its wearers.

I was disappointed in the appearance of the horses, but they are no doubt well suited to their work. The peculiar manner of riding of the Kossaks does not excite admiration, especially at a gallop, standing as they do almost upright in their stirrups. The custom of each regiment saluting the General with a shout is very striking. He replies to the effect that they have done well and that he is pleased with them; and they in return say, "We are glad to serve your Excellency and hope to serve you again." The step of the

KOSSAKS

infantry is almost as quick as that of the Italian "Bersaglieri."

The 14th of November—old style—is the birthday of the Empress Dowager of Russia. There was a grand service at the church, the whole of the garrison being called out in honour of the occasion. The Empress, sister of the Princess of Wales, is exceedingly popular. I have seen charming portraits of her in Russia, and regret that in England she is known only by photographs of an inferior description. We are so much accustomed to look upon the princesses of Hesse Darmstadt as more than half English, that it seemed strange to hear the lovely young Empress spoken of as altogether German. The title of Emperor is more commonly used than that of Czar. The title of "Czar" was borrowed by the Russians from the Tartars, who used it in addressing the Khans. It is an ancient Oriental word, as may be seen in the Slavonian translation of the Bible. It signifies in Persic a *throne* or *supreme* authority, and it is to be traced in the termination of the names of the Assyrian and Babylonish Kings, as Phalassar, Nabonassar, etc.

The courteous welcome of General Kuropatkin made the visit to Askabad very agreeable. Madame Kuropatkin invited the English travellers to a reception, and a dance was added at the cyclists' club. Bicycles are to be seen wherever the roads admit of their passing, but I did not see any Russian ladies cycling. The process of dressing for a ball in a railway carriage has the charm of novelty, but it is by no means easy of accomplishment.

The visit of the English travellers was understood to be one of pleasure only, and any allusion to politics would have been in the worst possible taste; but the prohibition laid upon excursions towards the south was obviously intended to check indiscreet curiosity as to the advance of Russia towards Afghanistan.

The departure of the train from Askabad was a sight not to be forgotten by those who were so fortunate as to be present on the occasion. The presence of the ladies of Askabad was felt to be a graceful compliment to their English sisters. The uniforms, now so well known to us, gave brilliancy to the scene, and the enlivening strains of the military bands allowed no time for regrets until the last moment when the engine steamed out of the station; the travellers, all grouped in the "Observation Car," cheered and waved handkerchiefs until their kind friends were lost to sight.

Dushak—meaning in Persian "two branches"—is the station farthest south on the line, and nearest to the Afghan frontier. From it on one side is the direct road south-east to Sarakhs and Herat; and on the other almost due south to Meshed and "Golden Khorasan," slice after slice of which is being annexed by Russia.

Khorasan, the "Country of the Sun," is rapidly becoming a Russian possession, and the best road to India is by way of Meshed,

Herat and Candahar. Khorasan has an area as large as that of Great Britain; Meshed, under Russian rule, would naturally become the capital town of the district which is said to be "a splendid country, with climate and soil suitable for European colonisation." "Englishmen are occasionally met with who question the strategetic value of Herat, but I have never encountered in the course of my Russian reading and travels any *Russian* disposed to speak lightly of the place." I quote from well-known writers whose warnings have been neglected in their own country, but whose sagacity has been proved in almost every point. The subject is painful to dwell upon. We may not approve the methods of the Russians nor their "careless handling of the truth," but we are forced to admire the magnificent success which they have achieved by their steady perseverance and tenacity of purpose.

General Kuropatkin, in his interesting little book on the Anglo-Russian frontier "*Les Confins Anglo-Russes dans l'Asie Centrale,*" complains of the desire of the English to establish a neutral zone, and of their presents of modern arms to the Amir of Afghanistan and other rulers with that intention. "Ces mesures ont pour but de rendre la zone neutre en question aussi impenétrable que possible aux Russes, *dans le cas où ceux-ci se trouveraient disposés à reculer plus au sud leurs frontières d'Asie.*"

In a recent conversation with a Russian gentleman, in no way connected with the army or with the diplomatic service, I expressed a hope that England and Russia would always remain the best of friends, united in their interests in the commerce of the East; but still it might be well to keep Afghanistan as a neutral state. He replied with a quiet smile, "Ah! but *we* don't think so." This simple remark showed the general feeling among his countrymen.

The Meshed (sepulchre) of Khorasan is the tomb of Imam Riza, and is the great place of pilgrimage of the sect of the Shiahs to which the Persians belong. They revere Ali, fourth

Khalif in succession to Mohammed and husband of his daughter Fatima, as the vicar of God, not inferior to the Prophet himself. They accept the teaching of the Koran only. The Sonnites or Sunni, the orthodox Musulmans, accept the Sonna (tradition), a collection of the laws or precepts of Mohammed handed down from his own *unwritten* words. They respect the memory of Abubekr, Omar, Othman and Ali, but assign the lowest degree of sanctity to Ali. There is much that is beautiful in the Koran, and every chapter is headed "In the name of the kind and merciful God." The dictates of gentleness and charity were soon forgotten by the terrible Mohammedan conquerors, and there were dissensions among them from the beginning of their history. Sympathy naturally goes with the gallant Ali, from his fourteenth year the faithful and devoted follower of his father-in-law. When he became Khalif, A.D. 656, he turned his arms against the rebel Moawiyah or Muawia, head of the family of Ommiades, who had assumed the title of *Amir* of the Faithful, pretended to avenge the murder of Othman, and was assisted, even on the field of battle, by Ayesha, the spiteful and vindictive widow of Mohammed. Ali, always generous in his impetuosity, proposed a single combat in order to save bloodshed; but his offer was refused, and after many disappointments and misfortunes he retired to Cufa, south of Bagdad, and fell by the poisoned dagger of an assassin. All the rulers of Persia down to Nadir Shah, A.D. 1743, have made splendid presents to the Tomb of Ali—Meshed Ali—near Cufa. Meshed Hossein, the sepulchre of his unfortunate son, is about thirty miles distant from that town. Hassan, his eldest son, retired to Arabia, but Hossein, the second son, inherited his father's spirit, and gathering his few but faithful followers he endeavoured to make good his claim as representative of the line of Hashem, the family of the prophet. Unfortunate like his father, Hossein was reduced to the direst straits, and being informed that he must submit as a captive to expiate his offences, during the short respite of a night he prepared with calm and solemn resignation to encounter his fate. He checked the lamentations of his sister Fatima, who deplored the impending ruin of his house.

"Our trust," said Hossein, "is in God alone. All things, both in heaven and earth, must perish and return to their Creator," etc. "He pressed his friends to consult their safety by a timely flight; they unanimously refused to desert their beloved master. On the morning of the fatal day he mounted on horseback, with his sword in one hand and the Korán in the other; his generous band of martyrs consisted only of thirty-two horse and forty foot. They fought desperately, a truce being allowed on both sides for the hour of prayer, and the battle ended with the death of the last of the companions of Hossein. Alone, weary and wounded, he seated himself at the door of his tent. As he tasted a drop of water, he was pierced in the mouth with a dart, and his son and nephew, two beautiful youths, were killed in his arms. He lifted his hands to heaven; they were full of blood, and he uttered a funeral prayer for the living and the dead. In a transport of despair his sister issued from the tent, and adjured the general of the Cufians that he would not suffer Hossein to be murdered before his eyes; a tear trickled down his venerable beard, and the boldest of his soldiers fell back on every side as the dying hero flung himself among them. The remorseless Shamer, a name detested by the faithful, reproached their cowardice, and the grandson of Mahomet was slain with three and thirty strokes of lances and swords. After they had trampled on his body they carried his head to the castle of Cufa, and the inhuman Obeidollah struck him on the mouth with a cane. 'Alas,' exclaimed an aged Musulman, 'on these lips have I seen the lips of the apostle of God!' In a distant age and climate the tragic scene of the death of Hossein will awaken the sympathy of the coldest reader. On the annual festival of his martyrdom, in the devout pilgrimage to his sepulchre, his Persian votaries abandon their soul to the religious frenzy of sorrow and indignation."

I have copied nearly word for word Gibbon's touching account of this tragedy; he adds that the two sepulchres are in the hands of the Turks, "who tolerate and tax the devotion of the Persian heretics." A feeling of repulsion takes the place of sympathy with the modern Shiahs, who, at this annual festival, cry aloud and cut themselves with knives after the manner of the heathen of old.

"The twelve Imams of the Persian creed are Ali, Hassan, Hossein, and the lineal descendants of Hossein to the ninth generation. The twelfth and last of the Imams, conspicuous by the title of *Mahadi*, or *the Guide*, surpassed the solitude and sanctity of his predecessors. He concealed himself in a cavern near Bagdad; the time and place of his death are unknown, and his votaries believe that he still lives and will appear before the day of judgment to overthrow the tyranny of the *antichrist*. It is singular that Mahometans should borrow this expression from the religion that they detest. The genuine and the fictitious descendants of Mohammed and Ali enjoy several privileges, and are entitled to wear the *green* turban, the colour of the prophet."

An Armenian guide, a Christian, corrected me one day when I spoke of the Persians as Musulmans, and said they were Shiahs, *i.e.*, Schismatics. I suppose that the Sonnites or Sunnites, the orthodox Turks, deny them the appellation of Musulmans (the saved). In most countries the Persian government is spoken of with contempt. A foreign diplomat is said to have remarked: "C'est le dernier des pays et le dernier des peuples." I have, however, heard charming accounts of the refinement and superior education of Persian ladies.

The railway to Merv turns north as it leaves Dushak with its lovely view of the distant mountains, and after crossing a tributary of the Heri Rud continues its way through fifty miles of dreary sands. I refrain from making any remarks about General Annenkoff's wonderful triumph over the difficulties of the Trans-caspian line of railway. This has been often and admirably described. The monotony of the desert gives one time to realize the tremendous labour that has been spent upon this route. No doubt those who worked became expert through the sameness of their occupation, with the result of a marvellous rapidity of execution, as is the case with the great Trans-Siberian Railway. That line can now be reached with ease from Calais or Paris direct, and offers much to please travellers in search of new scenes and little known countries, but the historic interest can never equal that of the road through Central Asia.

The first feeling on arriving at Merv is one of disappointment. We all know that it is the *new* town—so to speak—and not the mysterious "Queen of the World" that we must first visit, but still we peep out of the windows in the early morning hours expecting something more than the regulation railway station; the stations are all of one pattern, though not all are so well appointed as at Askabad. The single line has the great advantage of not obtruding modern innovations upon your dreams of the past, but the numerous sidings at the stations appear to irritable nerves to have been constructed chiefly for the accommodation of engines that are perpetually shrieking or letting off steam.

The English travellers were courteously received by General Spokoiski Franzevitch, who organised in their honour a very interesting sham fight. The general idea of the siege was similar to that at Askabad, with the difference that instead of an immense plain the ground was rough and broken. The blowing up of a mine made an effective finale, and gave the impression of something more than mimic warfare.

A spirit of friendship and goodwill animated both besieged and besiegers as they repaired to a high bank where they partook of a charming picnic luncheon. The scene I thought the most picturesque that I had ever witnessed. The strangers, with some of the ladies and officers from Merv, looked down upon a group of about thirty officers gaily refreshing themselves after the exertions of the morning and occasionally breaking into snatches of song. Uniforms of every description, groups of camels with natives interested in the proceedings, gave a touch of Oriental life that was quite fascinating. Loyal toasts as usual were proposed and duly honoured. A rather lengthy speech in English was forgotten in the pleasure given by one in which a Russian officer gracefully welcomed the visitors, poetically alluding to rumours of an invasion in the air; the rumours had indeed come true, but the invasion was not one of enemies but of good friends and fair ladies whom they were delighted to welcome.

The march past, after the festivities were over, took place in a dusty road; the General's position was on a bank, which made it exceedingly difficult for field officers to execute with

PICNIC AFTER SHAM FIGHT, MERV

neatness the rapid manœuvre to take up their position beside him as each regiment passed. The customary shout of the soldiers, as a salute to the General, seemed like five or six rough words having exactly the same sound. They marched remarkably well, but they were covered from head to foot with the terrible dust which is destruction to clothing of every description.

Before witnessing the review a visit was made to a Turkoman village, surrounded as usual by walls of baked mud. This village has some pretensions to importance as it contains a *medressé* or university. The students were absent, and several of their abodes were entered; most of them are like prison cells, and as they have no windows, study must be difficult in the imperfect light. Some have shelves with pretty wood carving and recesses under stalactite ornamentation. A bare empty building is used as a mosque. Some of the dwellings have handsomely carved wooden doors. The men in their best attire stood about doing nothing particular; they exert themselves only to look after their horses, and doubtless they would have been surprised to hear that they were less interesting than the despised women who were making felt and carpets with great dexterity and with no pattern before them. I was told that married women only work in this manner. They give a carpet for their daughters' dowries, and would never sell what they make for that purpose.

Some horses belonging to the Turkomans were exhibited, gay with elaborate trappings; they had broad engraved silver pieces on the reins, in some cases enamelled and adorned with large turquoises and other stones. In front of the chest the chief ornament consisted of a handsome boss, also of enamel or engraved and jewelled silver. Upon our arrival at the village, bread and salt were offered by the principal men of the tribe. A few miles farther at an unenclosed "*aul*" some native musicians, in honour of the visitors, discoursed anything but sweet music through cane pipes! They stood in a row, young men and old writhing to

MEDRESSÉ. TURKOMAN VILLAGE

the emotions they wished to inspire, bending backwards and throwing up their heads in their struggles to reach high notes. It was a painful exhibition, but gave evident pleasure to the bystanders. The English ladies were invited to enter a "kibitka," round which were seated in Oriental fashion about eight or ten women with whom they shook hands and who seemed pleased with the visit. Some of them wore many rings and bracelets and heavy ornaments on their heads and round their necks. It was amusing to notice their simple devices to draw attention to these decorations. I did not know how many were the wives of one Turkoman; as a rule the men of these tribes do not have more than two wives. The women are not veiled, but they wear a shawl over their heads which they can use as a veil for the lower part of their faces, and they seem to do so by an instinctive movement when men are present. They wear this kind of shawl sometimes over a high head-piece made of reeds which is peculiar to this part of the country. I felt sorry when the women were ordered to come out and arrange themselves in front of the kibitka to be photographed. Two of them probably ranked as beauties on the strength of their having very rosy cheeks and small sparkling eyes. They were certainly the only women with an approach to good looks that I saw during the time that I was in Central Asia. Alexander the Great's admiration for his beautiful Roxana (if indeed she was really of Turkoman origin) must have been an acquired taste; perhaps he was tired of the loveliness and delicate features of Greek and Persian beauties.

The roads leading to these villages and to the ground where the review was held were exceedingly rough, especially in the neighbourhood of some works for irrigation. I was in a carriage with a pair of splendid black Russian horses, only half broken. The lady sitting beside me did not appear to be aware of the danger, but the officer who accompanied us was evidently uneasy. The driver could scarcely

TURKOMAN WOMEN MAKING CARPETS

keep his control over the excited animals, and at the moment of starting from Merv there seemed to be a probability of our taking a plunge over the bridge into the Murghab.

This interesting day was brought to a close by a ball at the officers' club. I had heard that the dancing of the Russians was inferior only to that of the Austrians, but this opinion must have been the exaggeration of a Russophile! As to their hospitality there could be but one opinion.

It was a pleasure to watch the mazurka danced in a fashion very different from anything to be seen in England. The ladies take very small steps and fly the length of the room led by one hand; their partners, on the contrary, take very long strides backwards; they occasionally turn, as in a round dance, but apparently not according to any rule. It must be very fatiguing, but it is the custom in every dance for the gentlemen to change their partners several times. Literally a *tour de valse*.

The ball-room was very pretty seen from the

raised daïs where bonbons and chocolate were placed on tables decked with flowers for the ladies looking on or resting between the dances. The cotillon was long and not amusing; the most charming event of the evening was a Kossak dance between a lady and one of the officers, he feigning to attack her with a knife, she always evading him and gliding swiftly away with the short step peculiar to the dance; at last she allowed herself to be caught and the dance was ended by her captor gracefully kissing her hand. The supper at a Russian ball is a *serious* matter, if the word can be applied to so gay an affair. Russian officers are said to have strong heads, but they must have admitted that, on this occasion, Englishmen did full justice to their complimentary toasts, and yet returned to the ball-room to dance as lightly as before passing through the ordeal.

There is nothing worthy of notice in the new town of Merv; we require to be reminded of the fact that we are now in an *oasis*; the word suggests the idea of a green spot in a dry place. Here everything is shrouded in dust; the only proof of fertilization is the welcome appearance of the large sweet melons which delight even those who, like myself, have never before cared for them. This was the original home of oranges and lemons, peaches and apricots, figs and olives, vines, nuts and—queen of all flowers —the rose.

In my early days Moore's flowing verse had a charm for me that has lasted until this visit to a land that he never saw, but that he described so wonderfully. The very name of Murghab has a charm that is irresistible, and the charm is not destroyed by the reality of a dwindling stream, dwarfed by the uses of irrigation, and finally losing its diminished waters in the insatiable desert. The climate is very unhealthy, the soldiers suffer much from malaria and influenza.

Baïram Ali, ten miles farther by train, is the station for old Merv. The name commemorates the heroic life and death of a Persian chief beloved by his followers and by the inhabitants of Merv, whom he had for many years protected from the incursions of the robber tribes that infested the country. Women fought in the defence of Merv; but, deserted by other rulers in Khorasan envious of his fame, Baïram Ali Khan was overcome by the forces of the Amir Maasum of Buchara, who slew him and broke down the celebrated dam to which the country owed its fruitfulness. This was in 1787; the inhabitants were transferred to Buchara, where they still preserve their nationality and are known as Mervi. They had, indeed, been transported from far distant lands by the Persians, but under their rule the country was fertile and the people happy and prosperous.

European ideas of patriotism and devotion to the soil, for which our ancestors have fought and bled, must be altogether dismissed in the study of Oriental history. Russians, in the policy of transporting whole populations from one end to the other of their gigantic Empire, do but act in accordance with Eastern practices, which are better understood by them than by us. "In the East, instead of the gradual development of political systems we find only the personal substitution of ruler for ruler, of dynasty instead of dynasty, of nation instead of nation. A Western people, groaning under oppression, removes the tyranny itself by a Licinian Law, a Magna Charta, or an Oath of Rütli; an Eastern people never looks farther than to effect a personal change in the tyrant while the tyranny remains unchanged. So it happens that while all Western history is interesting and instructive—as the history of progress—large portions of Oriental history are alike unprofitable and impossible to be remembered. Here and there a hero or a monster appears on the scene, whose glory or whose crimes at once rivet our attention; the pure virtue of an Akbar and the splendid infamy of a Timur are as attractive as any personal narratives in the history of the West."

We approach the great "Queen of the

World" with tremulous curiosity; we desire to collect our thoughts, to keep in remembrance all that we know of her history—and how little it is. We are told that a city occupied by the Persians existed here before the arrival of Alexander the *Great*—first and most worthy to bear that title. Doubting spirits murmur that the name of "Iskander" is attached to every memorable spot in Eastern lands; but, knowing as we do the line of his march upon still more distant countries, there is no difficulty in believing that he did really visit this spot. Of all the great conquerors known to history, he is, in spite of dark stains upon his life, the most sympathetic, the most worthy of respect. Great generals as a rule are sure of the devotion of their followers. Alexander the Great shared the sufferings of his troops, and we read that, B.C. 331, after the defeat of Darius at the battle of Arbela, he built a town for the wounded or infirm soldiers of his armies—an act of charity rarely thought of before the Christian Era. He does not stand alone as a soldier calumniated by his countrymen sitting at ease at home. The king-hating Greeks, who rejoiced in the murder of Philip of Macedon, attributed to his son every vile passion that their malice could invent.

Beyond vague allusions to Bactria and Sogdiana, we hear little of the cities of Central Asia until the fifth century, when the Nestorians appeared and made so many converts that bishoprics were established at Merv, Samarkand, Kashgar, and other places. The heresy of Nestorius consisted in his denial of the union of the divine and human nature in the person of Our LORD, as taught by the Church. He had been patriarch of Constantinople in 428; he was a persecutor of his religious opponents both before and after his condemnation at the Council of Ephesus 431. In Persia the Nestorians put to the sword 7700 Catholics and Monophysites.

In the seventh century the great wave of the Saracen invasion swept over Asia. Persia was at this time considered the most refined and cultivated of all nations. Great was her fall when at the battle of Kadesia the unfortunate Yezdejird, grandson of Khosru II., was defeated by the Arab chief Khaled, "the Sword of GOD," the most merciless of his race. Yezdejird was only fifteen years old, and after another defeat he fled to the East, where he was kindly received by the princes of Ferghana and Samarkand, and finally took refuge with the Emperor of China, Taitsong, first of the dynasty of Tang.

Abubekr, Omar and Othman fought with Mohammed in person; but on succeeding in turn to the title of Khalif, each one had passed middle age and remained in Arabia, governing the people and receiving news of the victories of his lieutenants. They lived in the most frugal simplicity; a satrap of Persia, coming to do homage to Omar, found him asleep among the beggars on the steps of a mosque. The Khalif Othman promised the government of Khorasan to the first general who should enter that delightful province, and the standard of

Mohammed was planted in the cities of Merv, Herat and Balkh. Yezdejird returned to Merv in the hope of regaining his throne, but the faithless inhabitants turned against him and he was obliged to make his escape. A miller on the banks of the Murghab delayed him by haggling over the price of a boat to cross the river, and he was overtaken and killed—the last of the Sassanian kings of Persia. His two daughters married their captors, Hassan the son of Ali, and a son of Abubekr—such was commonly the fate of the wives and daughters of a conquered prince. For some time the Oxus remained the Turkish boundary, but under the Khalif Walid I., 705-715, the victorious camel-driver Kuteibe penetrated as far as China, taking possession of the rich cities of Buchara and Samarkand. We read of a valuable ornament dropped by a Turkish queen in her flight; and of jewels stolen from a Sogdian princess by the wife of Salem, the first Arabian woman who crossed the Oxus.

It is difficult to be exact about the dates of

the early conquests of the followers of Mohammed, because the Greek and Persian historians were naturally unwilling to record their own national disasters ; and the history of the Arabians was handed down by tradition only, until they settled in the cities of the conquered countries and studied their arts and literature ; they learnt much from the ancient civilization of China, and carried with them this learning to the farthest point of their western conquests in the Spanish peninsula. Moawiyah, A.D. 661, first Khalif of the Ommiades, made Damascus the seat of his government. The Abbassides founded the city of Bagdad, celebrated under its greatest Khalif, Harun al Raschid, the contemporary of Charlemagne.

There were sects among the Musulmans from the earliest times. In the eighth century the Arabs were divided into three factions. The Fatimites were known as the *green*, the Ommiades as the *white*, and the Abbassides, their bitterest enemies, as the *black*. Abu Moslem, a great general of this faction, took possession of Merv and drove away the last of the Ommiades, Obrahim, who died in a dungeon. Mervan, who would have been next in succession, was killed in Egypt, where there was a general massacre of that party, one only escaping to Spain where he became founder of the dynasty of the Ommiades.

In the tenth century there were three Khalifs independent of each other, whose capitals were at Bagdad, at Cairo and Cordova.

These terrible Arabian conquerors began all their dispatches and letters with the formula, "In the name of the most merciful GOD." They treated as brothers all who accepted their religion, and took tribute from those who declined to submit. The Jews were excepted from any toleration because of the personal rancour of Mohammed, who had expected that they would receive his teaching. In war these savage persecutors gave no quarter and expected none.

Mokannah or Hakim, the veiled Prophet of Khorasan, so well known to us in Moore's charming verse, appeared with his extraordinary pretensions between the years 770-779. It was in the always turbulent city of Merv that he tragically ended his life.

The fanatical zeal of the first followers of Mohammed had ended with their lives. After them the Arab hordes consisted of men who loved adventure for its own sake, and for the profitable occupation of plundering the *infidels*. They were succeeded by rulers who enjoyed the riches that they had appropriated, who lived in luxury, and were the greatest encouragers of the arts and sciences of their times.

Merv, as it was called by the Persians, or Meru by the Tartars, was one of the capitals of Khorasán. The rule of the Saracens ended there in 874. Like Buchara and Samarkand, it was the seat of a school of science and letters.

The "dark ages" of European history were also the dark ages of the East. Well known dates here and there help one to remember

OLD MERV

events that took place at the same time in both continents. It is interesting to note that a year before the birth of Mohammed, Alboin founded the Lombard Kingdom in Northern Italy; and fifteen years before he commenced to preach, St Augustine landed in England, A.D. 597. The Saracens plundered Rome in 837.

In the eleventh century, under the Seljuk Sultans, Merv was at the height of glory as "Queen of the World." By this time the Huns of Turkish origin had spread over Europe as far as Flanders, when Henry the Fowler and Otho the Great of Germany roused the spirit of the people and drove them back to Hungary. The ferocity of their incursions gave rise to the superstition that they were the forerunners of the Gog and Magog of Scripture. There was a general panic in Europe at the close of the tenth century, occasioned by the belief that the world was drawing to an end.

From the time of Harun al Raschid the

power of the Abbasside Khalifs of Bagdad declined until it existed only in name. They had introduced into their palaces Turkish troops from beyond the Oxus, who, like the praetorian guards in Rome, became in time their masters. In 934 a Turk was given the title of Amir al Omra—commander of commanders. The title became hereditary, and the position was much the same as that of the Mayors of the Palace in France.

In 997 Mahmud of Ghazna founded the dynasty of the Ghaznevides, and though nominally subject to the Khalif of Bagdad, reigned over the whole of the northern part of India. He waged war against the Gentus of Hindustan, destroyed their idols and temples, and everywhere established the religion of Mohammed. Mahmud was the first Musulman ruler who bore the title of *Sultan*, *i.e.*, lord and master. The record of his treasures is fabulous. He imprudently invited the Turkomans to cross the Oxus from Buchara and settle in Khorasan; they soon attacked him, and he was defeated and killed near Merv in 1038.

The Turkomans then chose for their leader Togrul Beg, the grandson of Seljuk, who at Samarkand had become a Musulman and died fighting against the *infidels*. The choice was decided by the divination by arrows, common in the East. A bundle of arrows inscribed with the names of candidates was presented to a child, and the owner of the name found on the arrow selected, was proclaimed chief.

Togrul Beg was a zealous Musulman. He obliged all the Turkish races to accept the Koran, but he ruled over his people with justice and moderation. He drove the Ghaznevides out of Khorasan, and faithfully supported the Khalif of Bagdad against the Fatimite Khalif of Egypt. The title of Sultan was bestowed upon him, and he was virtually ruler of the Moslem world. I am tempted to give at length the dramatic scene of the meeting of the Khalif and the Sultan from the pages of Gibbon. "The Turkish Sultan embarked on the Tigris, landed at the gate of Racca, and made his public entry on horseback. At the palace gate he respectfully dismounted and walked on foot, preceded by his Emirs without arms. The caliph was seated behind his black veil, the black garment of the Abbassides was cast over his shoulders, and he held in his hand the staff of 'the apostle of GOD.' The conqueror of the East kissed the ground, stood some time in a modest position, and was led towards the throne by the vizier and an interpreter. After Togrul had seated himself on another throne his commission was publicly read, which declared him the temporal lieutenant of the vicar of the prophet. He was successively invested with seven robes of honour, and presented with seven slaves, the natives of the seven climates of the Arabian Empire. His mystic veil was perfumed with musk; two crowns were placed on his head; two scimitars were girded to his side, as the symbols of a double reign over the East and West. After this inauguration the Sultan was prevented from prostrating himself a second time, but he twice kissed the hand of the Commander of the Faithful, and his titles were proclaimed by the voice of heralds and the applause of the Moslems. In a second visit to Bagdad the Seljukian prince again rescued the caliph from his enemies, and devoutly, on foot, led the bridle of his mule from the prison to the palace. Their alliance was cemented by the marriage of Togrul's sister with the successor of the prophet. Cayem, however, refused his daughter to the Sultan, disdaining to unite the blood of the Hashemites to the blood of a Scythian shepherd; and protracted the negotiations many months, till the gradual diminution of his revenue admonished him that he was still in the hands of a master. The royal nuptials were followed by the death of Togrul himself. As he left no children, his nephew, Alp Arslan, succeeded to the title and prerogatives of sultan, and his name after that of the caliph was pronounced in the public prayers of the Moslems."

Alp Arslan—*the valiant lion*—pushed his conquests westward and subdued Georgia and Armenia, but he could not induce the people to accept Islam. He defeated and took prisoner the unfortunate Emperor Romanus Diogenes near Erivan, 1071. The Emperor of the East was obliged to kiss the ground before the Turkish Sultan, who, however, treated him kindly, and after imposing terms of peace, set him at liberty. Alp Arslan returned to Khorasan to reconquer the home of his race at the head of a magnificent army, and attended by over a thousand princes; his glorious career was cut short by the dagger of a desperate chief whom he had condemned to death. The epitaph on his tomb at Merv has been often quoted—"Oh ye who have seen the glory of Alp Arslan exalted to the heavens, repair to Meru, and you will behold it buried in the dust!" The tomb, with its inscription, has entirely disappeared, and the knowledge that it once was here is perhaps even more striking than the sight of the shapeless ruins that in their gaunt deformity still look down upon the dust and ashes around them.

Alp Arslan was succeeded by his eldest son, Malek Shah, 1072-1092, who extended his dominions from the Chinese frontier to Arabia, and nearly to Constantinople. He was considered the greatest prince of his age; he encouraged arts and literature, and reformed the Kalendar in the Gregorian manner, calling it Gelalœan, *glory of the faith*, which was one of his titles. His end was inglorious; two years before his death his faithful vizier Nizam, an old man of ninety-three, lost his favour, and was killed by a fanatic—the first victim of Hassan Sebek or bin Sabah, founder of the Assassins, called by the crusaders the Old Man of the Mountain.

Malek Shah was called the Sultan of Persia. At his death his vast empire was divided into four parts, the most important being the Kingdom of Roum or Rum, with its capital at *Nice*, to the eternal shame of the Greek Christians.

Trebizond alone remained unconquered. In 1077, Jerusalem was taken by the Turks, who retained the city during twenty years, after which it fell into the hands of the Fatimite Khalifs of Egypt. These events took place about the time of the Norman Conquest of England.

I have wandered far from Merv, but it seems to me that to visit or to read about ruined cities without any distinct knowledge concerning their former inhabitants, is indeed to gaze upon "the dry bones of history." During my visit to Central Asia I was continually vexed at my inability to recall in proper order all that I had read about its history. The names of Saladin, who reigned from the Nile to the Indian Ocean, of Chingiz Khan and Tamerlane, are familiar to all; at Merv we are chiefly concerned with the terrible ravages of the Mongols. The line of Seljuk Turks ended with Sultan Sandjar, who, like his predecessors, made Buchara as well as Merv his capital. He built the celebrated dyke which was the means of irrigation for the oasis.

It is impossible to imagine a more tremendous scene of desolation than that which is presented by the present aspect of Merv. As far as the eye can see are shapeless heaps of ruins. The walls are in fairly good preservation with gateways that remind one of those of Rome, but within all is confusion; a few ruined mosques have the appearance of exaggerated height in their ghostly loneliness, where all around is crumbling dust. Owls are the only living creatures to be seen. I have heard that the sensitive had better refrain from turning over the sand here and in the desert, they might lose the comfort which they had enjoyed from the absence of pernicious insect life.

You are told that here are the ruins of three cities, but it is not reasonable to attempt any kind of classification. Again and again we read of the *total destruction* of the turbulent city, but then again and again we read of the resuscitated glory of the " Queen of the World."

There can never have been a *total* destruction, but after each catastrophe a new city must have partly covered and partly joined itself to the ruins of the last. The desertion of its inhabitants after the breaking up of the dam of the Murghab brought about the present absolute ruin. The distances between different points of interest are great. You cling to the sides of your carriage for safety as you gallop over what must have been the dwellings of human beings, possibly over dust that once had life and feeling.

The ruined mosques have in almost every case been lined with oblong tiles of beautiful turquoise blue enamel; so little remains *in situ* that, instead of adding to the beauty of the building now, they look forlorn and almost trivial, sticking to the walls here and there alone, or in ragged patches. Some of these tombs are places of pilgrimage for the Musulmans. The most important are two, side by side, called the Tombs of Standard-Bearers of the Prophet; they are in grey stone, well preserved, and having on them inscriptions from the Koran. Pilgrims attach pieces of their clothing to the tombs of martyrs or holy men of their faith. In this place, having finished their devotions, they leave behind them two rough tiles balanced together leaning towards each other, as a memorial of their visit, with the prayer that the days of greatness may be restored to them. Strangers ignorant of their meaning, or indifferent to such feelings, kick them aside. These tombs are partially sheltered by high walls, and from this spot we have the most extensive view of the city of the dead; truly it may be called the abomination of desolation. The destruction of Jerusalem only can have surpassed in horror the awful scenes of massacre, when, by order of Tuli Khan, son of the great Chingiz, the wretched inhabitants were driven out of their homes, by forty at a time, to a short distance outside the walls and there ruthlessly slain—men, women and children. Three or four hundred beautiful young girls were carried off as slaves, and about the same number of skilful workers in stone or metal, of Persian nationality, probably slaves in Merv, so that *they* would have only a change of masters. For generations Persians executed the beautiful designs that we see in the glazed tiles and other ornamental work throughout Central Asia. To be compelled to adorn the mosques and palaces of the hated *Sunnites* must have aggravated the bitterness of their servitude.

The mausoleum of Sandjar, last of the Seljuk Sultans, 1116-1157, is perhaps the most interesting ruin in Merv. The tomb is of plain stone, beside it is a long pole to which is attached the "Tong" (horse's tail), token that a great man or a warrior is buried on the spot. The lofty dome of imposing dimensions is supported by massive walls, cracked indeed, but adorned in parts with beautiful sculpture and blue and white enamel tiles. Legend says that the hero still sleeps, to return one day to restore the glory of his empire. Legend gives us the same idea in connection with Frederick I.

(Barbarossa) Emperor of Germany, 1152-1190. Poetry tells us that the widow of Sultan Sandjar, who dedicated this great work to his memory, placed his gift—a comb to adorn her head, now at his death bowed in grief—at the summit of the dome, where it will remain until the probable crash of an earthquake destroy the building, completing the work of devastation.

These pages of romance are pleasing, but they *leave us cold*, to use a French expression. Western sentiment cannot shake off the idea of "one life, one love," or, at least, one love at a time. Such histories, however, have in them a touch of softness which is welcome in this dismal place. One other spot rouses our sympathy; it is the comparatively modern tomb of a once celebrated doctor, a healer of men, resting in the midst of the destruction wrought by man; he lies beneath a sort of open canopy in the centre of a large enclosure, and great veneration is felt for his memory. Musulmans still believe that by passing under a low wooden arch close by, miraculous cures may be gained, and they leave there, as is customary, a portion of their garments—prayers must, naturally, accompany these acts of devotion. The singular custom of laying a closely folded shawl over a tomb is familiar to all who have visited Constantinople. The superstition concerning miraculous cures is more respectable than one common in England until recent times. "In the south-east part of the kingdom the country people split young ash trees, and make their distempered children pass through the chasm in hope of a cure. They have also a superstitious custom of boring a hole in an ash and fastening in a shrew mouse. A few strokes with a branch of this tree is then accounted a sovereign remedy against cramp or lameness in animals."

The three or four hours spent in old Merv seemed to me the most fatiguing that it has ever been my lot to endure. The sense of oppression of mind and body was intolerable. Clouds of penetrating dust irritated and stupified me at the same time. The objective world presented a vast area of desolation, a desolation so overwhelming that scarce one stone is left upon another; there is not even the outline of a human habitation, nothing but weird, shapeless mounds and great hollows, and over all this a thick pall of dust.

As we dashed back to the station at Baïram Ali a deep feeling of weariness that could not be shaken off made me almost insensible to the glory of one of the finest sunsets I have ever seen. My two companions must have been similarly impressed as silence fell upon us, broken only by some spasmodic remark that required no reply.

The railway to Tcharjui passes through about a hundred miles of the dreariest desert of dull coloured sand that can be imagined. It was the most difficult part of the line to lay, on account of the shifting sands. Travellers farther east in Turkestan have described sand-buried ruins, "one of them—a shrine, was first swallowed up, and again at a later date left free by the receding dunes." "A singular instance of this phenomenon has taken place in England on the Norfolk coast, where Eccles church was gradually submerged in sand. By 1839 the whole church was buried, by 1862 the tower reappeared, and in 1892 the sands cleared away on the landward side."

The sand dunes are mostly from ten to twenty feet high, but some are seen like little hills fully a hundred feet high, in some places higher. They cover the plain and follow in successive rows one behind the other, just like the marks left by wave ripples on a sandy beach, only on a large scale.

In the extreme east of Central Asia the sandy desert is found at its worst, and it is in connection with this quarter that most of the tales of weird horrors have their origin. How deeply the superstitious mind of the Asiatic may be impressed by these wastes of moving sands, and how little reason there is to wonder at the stories of ghosts, demons and visions with which he has invested the region, may

OLD MERV

be judged by General Prejevalski's vivid description of it. "The effect of these bare yellow hillocks," he writes, "is most dreary and depressing when you are among them and can see nothing but the sky and the sand; not a plant, not an animal is visible, with the single exception of the yellowish-grey lizards which trail their bodies over the loose soil and mark it with the patterns of their tracks. A dull heaviness oppresses the sense in this inanimate sea of sand. No sounds are heard, not even the chirping of a grasshopper, the silence of the tomb surrounds you."

The Chinese call the desert of Gobi "*A dry sea.*" Hinen Tsang's description differs little from that of the Russian traveller. "These sands," he says, "extend like a drifting flood for a great distance, piled up or scattered before the wind. There is no trace left behind by travellers, and oftentimes the way is lost, and so they wander hither and thither quite bewildered, without any guide or direction. So travellers pile up the bones of animals as beacons. There is neither water nor herbage to be found, and hot winds frequently blow. When these winds rise, both man and beast become confused and forgetful, and then they remain perfectly disabled. At times, sad and plaintive notes are heard and piteous cries, so that between the sights and sounds of this desert, men get confused and know not whither they go. Hence there are so many who perish on the journey. *But it is all the work of demons and evil spirits.*"

" If the superstition of the Asiatic is moved by the mystic scenes of the desert, his cupidity is also stirred by the legends of buried riches which the submerged cities are supposed to contain. Traditions lose nothing from age or from being often repeated, and the stories of hidden treasures are ancient enough to acquire a very strong influence on members of the population. From time to time, ornaments, vessels, images and coins of great interest are unearthed, but their value to the finders, whose only interest is in the worth of the metal they are made of, can scarcely be great. Perhaps the only systematic exploitation of the ancient sites ever undertaken, was that of Mirza Abà Bakr, Amir of Kashgar, about the end of the fifteenth and beginning of the sixteenth century, and we may infer nearly everything that was of intrinsic value was brought to light, while much that was of antiquarian interest was destroyed, so that when, at some future time, civilized explorers come to investigate the ruins, they will find little to reward their labours." I have gathered several of these interesting descriptions from the delightful "Tarikh-I-Rashidi," translated by Professor Denison Ross for Mr Elias.

These remarks do not apply to Merv; we must hope that before long the Russians may be roused to interest themselves in the history of the wonderful city and find time to unearth the treasures at their feet.

Shortly before arriving at Tcharjui, the frontier of the territory of the Amir of Buchara is passed. The Beg of Tcharjui, a splendid specimen of an Oriental prince, is full of gracious courtesy combined with calm dignity of bearing. His magnificent costume of dark blue velvet, elaborately embroidered with gold, would crush a man of inferior personal advantages, but with him it appears perfectly natural. His invitation to witness the national sports was gladly accepted by the English travellers. They were hospitably entertained in a large tent erected on high ground facing an immense open plain.

After the introductions were made and tea and sweetmeats offered, the stately Beg gave the signal for the games to begin. The "Baïga" gives great enjoyment to the people and to the horsemen who take part in it. The object of the riders is to secure the body of a decapitated goat which is thrown in their midst; they stoop down to the ground, but never dismount. The *mêlée* reminds one of polo, but on a very rough scale, and the poor horses must suffer severely in the stuggle; the interesting moment is when the most skilful player grasps his woolly prey and gallops away across the plain, followed by hundreds of his competitors, mostly riding admirable horses that appear to have as much English as Arab blood. I was surprised to hear that they were used for ordinary working purposes. The scene was brilliant beyond description and made one realize that this was an Eastern land, far removed from European ways and customs. The Bokhariots are infinitely superior in appearance to the Turkomans, whose features, or rather absence of marked features, suggest degradation of character and habits; the black sheep-skin head-dress in no way softens their coarseness, and the red and black or pink and black striped "dressing-gown" tied in at the waist, has always lost its freshness. The Bokhariots are generally tall and look dignified in their white turbans and picturesque "Khalats." Their dashing skill in riding contrasts singularly with their impassive and provokingly apathetic demeanour at other times. I began to wonder if they lost in childhood all ideas of fun or merriment, until one day on the road to Buchara, I saw two young men riding donkeys through a shallow pool, splashing each other and then racing along the dusty road with shouts of laughter. It is the only instance I can recall of any departure from gravity in public.

The sport of the Baïga became wearisome after three or four goats had been contended for. I believe there were six or eight in all. The winner of the goat must succeed in distancing all competitors and laying the much battered prize at the feet of the Beg. The grand excitement of the wild gallops over the desert was interrupted by the ugly rush of struggling men and horses, shouting, screaming, and belabouring each other with blows to the very verge of the tent under which we stood. A few races which followed gave us a better opportunity of appreciating the quality of the horses. They are generally larger than Arabs and have shoulders that speak of good action and steady walking pace, but I have read that the Turkomans ride on a journey at a peculiar fast walk that must be something like ambling. They are devoted to their horses and spare no trouble in training them, though they do not seem to love them as an Arab does his horse; but then one cannot imagine a Turkoman loving anything. I was told afterwards that General Alikhanoff had introduced many English horses into his stables. The general's name is a Russianized form of "Ali Khan."

An altogether disagreeable but favourite spectacle in this country is the "Batcha," a dance by boys in the dress of girls. They move about in a monotonous way, pretending in an affected manner to play with the pieces of long hair attached to the sides of their heads; and then suddenly they begin waltzing on their knees, or turning extraordinary somersaults. One felt ashamed to see three old men sitting on their heels in the blazing sun, while they played an irritating "tom-tom" as an accompaniment to the two dancing boys; the twanging sound haunted one's memory for days. The only thing to be done was to look far beyond them across the desert to the sand hills which had the appearance of distant mountains.

The weather was glorious, and the heat equal to that of a summer day in England. I felt that I could not gaze long enough at the wonderful scene before me; beautiful horses, riders gaily clad in every colour of the rainbow, not in subdued "artistic shades," but in brilliant reds, yellows, violets, greens that somehow did not clash, but charmed the eye.

An elaborate luncheon was served in the tent; mutton "pilau" or "ploff," as usual preponderating, with an endless variety of sweets. An excellent Russian band played outside, chiefly operatic music. A particularly good selection from "Faust," more often heard in Paris than in London, delighted me. It included the exquisitely beautiful overture, and the act of the Walpurgiss Nacht.

The Beg, like all strict Musulmans, neither drinks wine himself nor offers it to his guests.

Some of the ladies present expressed a great preference for the pale and highly-sweetened tea that took the place of stimulants, but some, I think, would have preferred a more exhilarating beverage after the fatigue and excitement of the day. The gentlemen showed signs of depression, and did not deny that their thoughts wandered to the ample supply of whisky with which they had provided themselves before leaving Constantinople.

The number of carriages being limited, I left the tent on foot with a young Polish lady and an officer to regain the station only a few hundred yards distant. We had scarcely started on our walk when our gallant host overtook us in his carriage, instantly alighted, and sent his equerry to insist upon our driving back to our travelling quarters. His horse was sent for, and magnificent he looked upon a superb charger, richly caparisoned with velvet and gold embroidery and jewels. It was the only opportunity I had of seeing an Eastern prince on horseback.

The Beg accepted an invitation to tea with the travellers in the open car at the end of the train. The time of his visit seemed long from the impossibility of conversing in a language known to the English as well as to the Bokhariots. It is to be hoped that the Beg will not form his opinion of the manners and customs of Western nations, and of Great Britain in particular, from his observations on this occasion. Several of his hosts appeared to forget the respect due to his rank and the courtesy due to a guest, especially to one who had exerted himself to make their visit to his country as agreeable as possible.

Tcharjui has been known from the earliest times under different names, such as Ammya, Amol, Gihon, etc. At the distance of about six miles is the new town, or rather settlement, near the great river Amu Daria, the Oxus of ancient history, which formerly ran into the Caspian Sea, but now empties its waters into the Sea of Aral. Ancient writers have attributed this change to violent volcanic action.

Legends affirm that the Oxus takes its source in Paradise. Innumerable are the historical recollections connected with the great river, but the name of Alexander is prominent before all others. The spot at which he forded it is rather higher up than the site of the modern bridge. The celebrated wooden railway bridge is a wonderful achievement among the many wonders accomplished by the Russians. Its length is over two thousand yards. There is a plan under discussion for diverting the waters of the Oxus from their present channel into their original course, but the enormous expense will probably prevent any serious consideration of the idea for a long time to come. Money is wanted for the *Oxus flotilla*, of which we have heard so much, and which from small unobtrusive beginnings has increased by yearly additions until, without the trouble of annexing the country, the Russians have gained between three and four hundred miles of territory, and have brought their direct water-way communication to the foot of the Hindu Kush.

Kossaks protect the banks of the river; shallow draught steamers and boats, like the native "Kayüks," encounter no difficulties. The Kohja branch of the Oxus is navigable as far as Faisabad, the capital of Badakshan; in favourable seasons so far even as Sebak. Karki and Khelif are important positions on the river; Khelif has a large Russian garrison, and commands the road to Balkh. Panj, the northern branch of the Oxus, is also in the hands of the Russians, and encircles the Badakshan country.

Buchara was once in possession of this territory and, when convenient to his advisers, the Amir will lay claim to it. Badakshan is mountainous but fertile. It has been celebrated in verse by Persian poets, who allude especially to its ruby mines in the neighbourhood of the Oxus which were worked by the chief of Kunduz. The rubies are found in round pieces of pebble or flint and imbedded in limestone. Chitral commands almost every pass over the Hindu Kush, as Herat does over the Paropamissus Mountains. Why does not England occupy these posts? Seeing Afghanistan on the map we imagine that the inhabitants are a united people; but Herat hates its present rulers. It might as well belong to Persia as Badakshan to Buchara.

Merv would have been a troublesome possession for the English. It was natural that the Russians should add it to their conquests in Central Asia, but they *protested too much* against any such intention. Immediately after the taking of Khiva, the Emperor Alexander II. unnecessarily assured the world in general, and Great Britain in particular, that he did not intend to occupy the Khanate *permanently*. After the taking of Samarkand, 1881, the Amir of Buchara was assured that that town would be restored to him. England is pledged to maintain the integrity of Afghanistan, but Russia does not want to believe in any durable arrangement of frontier. It was said in 1885 : " If Russia had no designs on Herat, she would not care whether her frontier were at Sarakhs or Pul-i-Khatum, or at Yolat or Pendjeh." England appears to be the only country to undervalue the importance of Russia's advance in Persia, and to be blind to the real meaning of *scientific investigations* protected by Kossaks. The British Government has provided a safe and profitable road for Indian commerce with Buchara, starting from Quettah, passing through Beluchistan, in order to avoid the outrageous tariff imposed in Afghanistan, and ending at Seistan, a town within the Persian frontier. We now hear that Russia is displaying great interest and activity in this quarter of the "dying nation." Every effort has been made to induce the Hindu merchants to trade only with Russian firms, to the extent of offering them advances of money without interest, and there are rumours that the importation of indigo from India will be prohibited. Still later comes the information that, without a word of protest Russia has been allowed to obtain from Persia the right of a port at Enzeli, on the southern shore of the Caspian Sea; and that a road, or railway, protected, of course, by Kossaks, is being constructed to the Persian, or shall we anticipate and say, the *Russian* Gulf at Bender Abbas.

The Russian operations in Central Asia began with the subjugation of the Khirghiz tribes, followed by the conquest of Khokand, with the systematic establishment of a chain of fortresses on the Syr Daria (Jaxartes) communicating with the steamers on the Sea of Aral ; in the same manner as has now been done on the Oxus. Tashkend—a prize of great value—was added in 1855, after *assurances* that Russia had no designs of conquest, again followed by *assurances* that the farthest point necessary to insure success in the interest of good order and civilization had been reached. Buchara, in the eyes of all Musulmans, was the centre of religion, " holy Buchara "—" In other lands light falls upon the earth—from Buchara light rises to Heaven." Dissension among all the tribes of Central Asia was Russia's opportunity, and who would regret her march of victory if in her train she proclaimed liberty of commerce to all nations and peace within her borders; but it is not so, the latest example that suggests the expression "Punica Fides" is the policy of Russia in the Far East, the result of which will be disclosed in the near future.

Russia treats Orientals in Oriental fashion. The moderation of England is looked upon as weakness. We, in England, ignorantly look upon Russia as a European country, and as such, a civilizing power. Travellers tell us that the civilization of the masses in Russia is lower than that of the Asiatic tribes; should that be true it is difficult to see what advantages to these people themselves can accrue from their incorporation into the Great Muscovite Empire.

" Russifying Russia is to be continued until the Empire presents to the eye a single and harmonious whole. The group of able and resolute men who surround the Czar have decided that there is weakness in privileged states, weakness even in separate religious sects. The process of, so far as possible, compelling every Russian subject to give up his nationality and to become in outward form a member of the Orthodox Church has been going on for years, but in this country is misinterpreted; all who owe loyalty to the Czar are to be forced into a single mould."

Russia is treating her gradually acquired possessions with the barbarity of the conquerors of the so-called " dark ages" of Christianity; but her attacks are not upon uncivilized pagan lands, but upon some countries of higher and more ancient civilization than her own. The case of the unhappy Finlanders is imperfectly understood in England; but we cannot withhold from them our sympathy in their patriotic efforts to preserve their nationality and their ancient liberties.

" England has many enemies, or perhaps we might better say, many enviers." We do not pretend to be free from faults and to make no mistakes, but the wrong-doings of English men are detested and blamed in their own country. No one ever thinks of excusing a misuse of power, the contrary sentiment is pushed to excess. Sympathy with the weak and suffering makes the British public stupidly ready to blame those who from personal knowledge and experience have thought well to put down disaffection and mutiny with a high hand. We can hardly imagine that an excess of severity has ever been blamed at Petersburg.

The great wooden bridge over the Oxus is not beautiful, but it is not likely that it can be replaced by one of stone on account of the shifting sands; Tcharjui was once situated on its banks, and the river may again change its course. The works of the *flotilla* are about half a mile from the station; there is little to be seen; otherwise, strangers would probably not have been allowed to walk down there.

The river Oxus is one of the great points of interest to which one looked forward in thinking of all the wonders of Central Asia. The reality of a wide expanse of dirty, yellow-brown water is slightly disappointing. In spite of appearances it is wholesome to drink, and carries with it the fertilization that makes its possession so valuable to the Russians.

The train passes slowly and carefully over the long bridge, and during the time of transit —rather less than twenty-five minutes—the traveller has ample leisure to note from the observation car the great difficulty of this achievement. There is very little current near the western bank, and you become accustomed to the creaking of the wooden structure before you reach the exact passage of the mighty stream and are considerately informed that this is the really dangerous part of the bridge! Great precautions are taken against fire, and smoking is not allowed. In ordinary circumstances the waste of water must be exceedingly ugly with mud banks and islands, but on this occasion it was lighted up with the marvellous reflections of a glowing sunset, giving it the appearance of a sea of fire. It was difficult to turn away and leave the open car, but a penetrating chilliness came over the atmosphere, very trying after the extreme heat of the day at Tcharjui. These strong alternations of temperature were very remarkable; but as the season is usually one of constant rain, there was no excuse for complaint.

Nightfall prevented any observation of the fertile country through which the train passes to Buchara, which was reached, I think, in about five or six hours. Kara Kul is one of the stations on the line; it is famous for the best sheep skins of Central Asia. The Turkomans, no doubt, provide themselves here with their great head-pieces, but I was disappointed in the quality of the lambs' wool in the bazaars of Buchara and Samarkand. The choicest skins are probably dispatched to the European markets.

The new Russian town of Buchara is as yet uninteresting, but the railway will soon make it an important station; and that fact will perhaps preserve from vulgarization the truly Oriental city " Buchara es Sherif"—Bokhara

MEDRESSÉ AND TOWER, BUCHARA

in Central Asia

the Noble. A drive of ten miles brings us to the old town, in which perhaps is centred the greatest interest of a journey that is altogether interesting. Now we are really in an Eastern land, and leave far away all signs of modern civilization.

I must admit that I found the long drive very tedious. I had heard much of the fertility of the country, and certainly on each side of the road there were proofs of irrigation, but all was covered with a thick veil of dust—the most cruel dust that I have ever encountered. I observed in it a great peculiarity, it appeared to cover one's clothing with *splashes* of dust, and I was greatly interested to read in a French critique on the travels of M. Sven Hedin, the celebrated Swedish explorer, that he had noticed this appearance in the desert; he says: "on pouvait voir les grains de sable voler dans les airs et retomber sous forme de petites vagues." The only objects free from dust were the innumerable crows that were to be seen on the small leafless trees and all over the fields; their plumage was as glossy as that of a raven, and, as most of them are black and white, I at first supposed that they were magpies. I was told that their purpose in life is equivalent to that of the dogs in Constantinople.

The weather was delightful, but a cloudless sky in these lands does not mean "an Italian sky." There is never the clear brilliant sun of Italy. The air was softer than I have ever known it in that favoured land in the month of December, excepting sometimes in Rome, but there is always a kind of *haze* in the atmosphere which is unlike anything to which we are accustomed in Europe. The word is too strong to convey the idea, it is something difficult to explain.

The Amir of Buchara had not been seen in his capital for more than three years. He paid the English travellers the compliment of sending an escort of his own bodyguard to conduct them to the city and to assist them to visit the particular points of interest. These guards,

"Djigites," are all picked men, tall and imposing, wearing large white turbans, and *Khalats* of silk, purple and amber, red and gold-colour or red and white of different designs, or rather of no stiff design, but as if one liquid colour had been thrown with a large splash upon another. I observed that the larger the turban, the more dignified was the appearance of the wearer. For some time before arriving at Buchara, we have on our right a wide-spreading cemetery, which might be passed unnoticed in its shroud of clay-coloured dust, but here and there a long pole bearing a horse's tail marks the last resting-place of a warrior or an eminent man, and we become aware that the rounded mounds are the graves of the dead. I was told that the bodies are enclosed in these mounds, not underground, and that in summer this road is pestilential. Untroubled by such considerations I endeavoured to realize the marvellous actualities of the situation. Protected by a brilliant escort of the Amir's personal guards or police, a small party of

British subjects was actually about to enter the mysterious city whose precincts had been severely guarded from the approach of the *unbeliever* until it fell, crushed in the stern grip of the Eagle of the North. Few Englishmen have penetrated within its sun-dried walls, and one feels oppressed by recollections of heroic daring and tragic deaths, some of which may truly be called martyrdoms.

The town is surrounded by a high wall of baked clay and entered by great gates. The first feeling is one of disappointment; the houses are but one story high and seem to have no windows. The same dull clay-colour is over everything. We pass several mosques with pretty little minarets and graceful arches with delicately coloured enamel tiles, but all out of repair. When the bazaar is entered there is no longer any disappointment. It is a wonderful scene of Oriental life. Carriages seem out of place in the narrow winding streets, if such they may be called, and it is more interesting to wander about on foot, gazing at objects altogether strange in shape and colour. Above all, it is interesting to study the inhabitants at home, following their ordinary occupations in life. The merchants sitting in the usual manner in the open fronts of their shops or stores, apparently unmoved by any curiosity as to your intentions in examining their goods; never bringing out of their own accord fresh things to tempt you; always asking about three times the amount they mean to accept, and expecting you to sit down and haggle over the price for the amusement of the idle bystanders, who frequently proffer their advice on the subject. The Amir's guards occasionally turned round and dispersed the crowd; indeed, their arbitrary disposal of the population, turning back all who came across our path, whether riding or walking, was rather embarrassing; but it would have been impossible to thread our way alone through such a labyrinth. The awnings, which cover over the greater part of the bazaar, give a kind of darkness that is oppressive, something like the sensation of an approaching thunder-storm.

It is strange to feel frequently a gentle push against your back or shoulder, and turning round you see a patient little donkey, generally white, ridden by a native whose feet nearly touch the ground on each side; he may have a boy mounted behind him, or a dark blue or black bundle that represents a wife, her eyes and features completely concealed by the ugly black veil that women in Buchara wear over their faces. Or there may follow the rider two or three camels tied one after another. All your attention is required to get out of the way, especially if at the same time you happen to meet a cart with two great wooden wheels over ten feet high. The cry of warning is "pusht" or "poisht," I have heard it pronounced both ways, and should the rider be young or impatient you must step briskly aside. Accidents do not appear to occur and perfect order is kept. It is considered beneath the

THE TOWER OF BUCHARA
L

dignity of a Bokhariot to walk, but Jews are not allowed to ride.

The lofty tower of Buchara, about two hundred feet high, ornamented with brickwork in bands of different designs, is one of the most beautiful monuments in Central Asia and is in perfect preservation; at the top is a stork's nest. Thanks to Russian civilization, it is no longer the place of execution for criminals, who until lately were thrown from its summit into the market-place, to be dashed to pieces before a ferocious and admiring populace. This dreadful form of punishment was not peculiar to Buchara; we read in the Bible that the sons of Judah brought their prisoners to "the steep of a certain rock and cast them down headlong from the top, and they were all broken to pieces." The Tarpeian Rock is familiar to all visitors to Rome, but nothing makes one realize the horror of the scene in the same way as does the sight of this wonderful tower. Torture is no longer permitted by the Russians, and the terrible pit full of vermin, into which our gallant countrymen Captain Conolly and Colonel Stoddart were thrown in 1842, has been closed for ever. Dr Wolff tells us that these gentlemen might have saved their lives had they consented to deny their faith. Slavery also, by the influence of the Russians, has been abolished. The prisons still in use are a disgrace to humanity. The overcrowded cell for ordinary prisoners is nearly dark. The miserable creatures condemned to death, or to imprisonment for life, wear an iron collar with a chain which fastens them in a row to each other and to the wall; there is no hope of release but by death, either natural or by the hand of the executioner. Tobacco and good bread, or trifles of a like nature may be offered them, but in small quantities for fear they should be deprived of them by their gaolers.

Buchara of modern days has been described as the worst haunt of vice and murder in Asia. I expressed to a Russian officer disgust at the odious cruelties under the rule of the Amir, and a wish that, like the Khan of Khiva, he

PRISONERS OF BUCHARA

might be deprived of all independent authority; but I was given to understand that his great wealth is useful for the purposes of government for the present, and that he is not allowed to indulge in any barbarous acts of tyranny.

Russia's advancing "torch of civilization" has already cleared out many frightful and degrading abuses of power. With that we must rest satisfied, and certainly in other hands the great Oriental city would lose its fearsome and strange fascination, its life that is so totally different from all that is European.

Buchara and Merv were always rivals in worldly things, but "the *Holy City*" was at all times the central point of the social and hierarchical life of Central Asia. The reputation for learning and enlightenment was shared with the towns of Samarkand and Kashgar.

Buchara is a city of mosques, schools, and medressés — *universities*. It is strange that they should all be allowed to fall into ruin while still in use. They are lavishly ornamented with enamel tiles, but the delicate designs lose all their beauty from the falling away of the greater part of the pattern in every building. The rooms of the students are mere cells, but some of them have artistic ornamentation, carved shelves of wood with inlaid work, and niches with stalactite vaulting. The large pools in front of the mosques, for purposes of ablution before prayer, are exceedingly unpleasant to approach, and it is not surprising that the people who will drink of their water are afflicted with a disgusting, if not always dangerous disease. This is especially the case in the Righistan, or great market-place. It is the most crowded part of the city, though the open bazaars are less attractive than in the richer quarters. It is the market particularly for fruit and vegetables.

Not far from the Righistan is the Citadel, the palace of the Amir, built by Alp Arslan, 1063. The great entrance, added by Nadir Shah, 1739, frowns down upon the town from a lofty eminence. Within it are several public offices, and just inside the gateway was the horrible vermin pit. Admission is not granted to strangers. Nadir Shah, a Turkoman shepherd boy, rose to the highest power and revived the glory of the Persian Empire. Mahmud, the Afghan usurper, trusting to Russian promises of help, had ceded the Caspian provinces; but Nadir supported Prince Tamasp, the rightful heir, and was eventually proclaimed Shah. He penetrated into India through Afghanistan, took possession of Delhi with a spoil of the value of £30,000,000, and then turned his arms against the Usbeg princes of Khiva and Buchara. The Turkoman tribes of Merv looked upon him as one of their own race and offered no opposition; they were rewarded by a season of great prosperity, ending with the fatal ruin of their city, so bravely defended by Baïrum Ali. It was on this occasion that the revengeful Bokhariots broke down the celebrated dyke that was the pride of Merv; since that time the doomed city has been punished for its crimes and treacherous dealings by the successive sieges by Bokhariots, Afghans, Persians (after their capture of Saraks, 1833), and finally by the Russians.

To return to Buchara. A notable point in the great gate of the Citadel is the clock made as the price of his life by an Italian for the atrocious Nasrullah, the Amir who murdered the two brave English officers.

The custom of throwing prisoners into a pit has been common in the East from the earliest ages. We all remember that Daniel was cast into the den of the lions, and also that Jeremias was "let down by ropes into the dungeon, where there was no water but mire. And Jeremias sank in the mire." In an enclosed shed opposite to the gateway of the Citadel or Ark are some strange specimens of old guns with mouths shaped like dragons and other monsters.

In visiting the different points of interest in Buchara, you cross and re-cross the great covered bazaar, vainly endeavouring to remember a way by which you have already

CITADEL OR ARK, BUCHARA

passed. It is like an ever-changing kaleidoscope, brilliant colours, picturesque robes, constant movement in the streets, and cross-legged apathetic merchants, with the inevitable cup of tea beside them, planted in the midst of their wares on each side of the streets, looking precisely as their forefathers must have looked when Master Anthony Jenkinson spent two months here in the reign of Queen Elizabeth, and also at the time of the visits of the eight or ten Englishmen known to have been in the city before the occupation by the Russians. The effect is as if you were in a dream or taking part in some wonderful scene at a theatre, and this is increased by the fatigue of walking for hours over the very uneven and dusty thoroughfares, where the sounds of *traffic* are completely deadened, while there is in the air a ceaseless hum of human voices mingled with the cries of boys selling sweetmeats on trays hanging from their necks, or the startling "poisht" warning you of the leisurely but formidable approach of a huge camel, squaring his elbows and proceeding on his way with a supercilious air that is most diverting when you feel yourself to be in safety. There are open kitchens in almost every street, where Bokhariots can buy at any time freshly cooked kabobs and various kinds of bread, in an atmosphere redolent of fat mutton.

Strangers do not excite much interest. Some heavily-veiled women occasionally turned to look, and whispered to each other their impressions concerning the bold women who walked in public with their faces uncovered. Their remarks upon the practical, but certainly not picturesque costumes of our countrymen, can hardly have been more flattering. I occasionally perceived a black look of hatred or contempt, but there was no *sign* of ill-will, and in making by myself some small purchases, I observed that I obtained what I wanted for a more reasonable price than when I applied for help to the magnificent guide in deep purple and amber *Khalat* who directed my wanderings. He was certainly a model of patience, and endeavoured to transact business for me in the manner of the country, which was impossible to reconcile with my hatred for bargaining. When I was offered a wooden frame with rows of big beads to mark the price, I altered the number to what I considered right, and declined further conversation on the subject. But my plan was not one to be recommended to those who had patience to go through the usual process of haggling. The quarters occupied by silk merchants and metal workers were those that I particularly wished to see. I was disappointed in the quality of the silks, but the busy workshops of brass and copper are truly delightful. The *kungana* — ewers of chiselled copper — are quite irresistible; they have beautiful designs in black or brown and dull gold-colour, and they are usually sold with a tray of a similar pattern. The shapes are very good, though not exactly what is called "classical"; the handles lack the bold upward spring of the Etruscan vases, but they have a style of their own, and it is very interesting to watch the process of cutting or chiselling.

The Buchara embroidery in large designs in wool or silk on coarse linen is perfectly charming, and I brought home several pieces for use as portières, or for throwing over couches. The old pieces are superior in colouring to the new, on account of the deterioration in modern dyes. They are worked by young girls, who never continue their occupation after marriage. For this reason you will often find that a spray or a flower has been left unfinished, which adds interest to your purchase. Pretty ornaments and *bibelots* in enamel work are peculiar to Buchara, and turquoises may be had for very low prices, but they have no attraction for connoisseurs. Russians value only such stones as have the cabichon form.

Luncheon, the two days that I spent in Buchara, was by order of the Amir offered to the English travellers in the "Palace of the Ambassadors," a dreary place entered through a courtyard and garden. The repast was excellent, though rather lengthy, and upon the first occasion tea only was provided as a beverage. The kind forethought of our Polish pioneer supplied on the second day refreshment of a kind more suited to Western ideas and habits. Fortunately, at the time, I did not know that the former owner of the house, having offended his master, was by his order walled up and starved to death in his own dining-room!

At the Ambassador's Palace a well-known French lady, a great traveller, accepted the hospitality offered her. She had accomplished without molestation a wonderful journey through Siberia, and was returning home by Central Asia. I was told that she had the intention of publishing her "Souvenirs de Voyages en Orient," and, should her powers of description be equal to her charm of manner and conversation, a most delightful book will be the result. I walked back with her from the bazaar, and she told me that she had been assisted beyond her expectations at every stopping place on her route. She was, of course, provided with papers from Petersburg, where, from her nationality, she would be *persona grata*

There is a hospital for lepers near Buchara. The unhappy sufferers from this disease are allowed to beg in parts of the city, but there is no outward indication of their malady, excepting that the women are unveiled. Poor creatures, they escape at least the feeling of suffocation which their sisters must endure behind their hideous stiff black coverings.

The Amir of Buchara possesses a summer palace, surrounded by high walls of clay, about half way between the railway station and the old town. It must be an agreeable residence in hot weather; the gardens are extensive, they have running water beside the paths, and flowering shrubs are trained over the trellis borders and arches. There are fountains to cool the air and give refreshment from the dust outside. I saw a few fine specimens of the hideous broad-tailed sheep, the pride and joy of the Turkoman tribes. The building has no architectural interest; the exterior is plain and the windows are painted to represent white curtains, in execrable but undoubtedly fashionable taste. I remarked the ridiculous idea repeated in many places. A very fine design of decoration in the frieze of a wall in the same courtyard was absolutely provoking by way of contrast. The carpets in the audience or throne room were perfect in colouring and in richness of effect, the ceilings good and handsome, the walls screamingly ugly in crude reds and blues. Behind the gilt throne were three papered panellings, two might have come from a good London house, the other was absurdly incongruous. At the farther end of the room was a charming arrangement of marble columns and a fountain, suggestive of bathing purposes *à la* Alma Tadema, but probably used only for luxurious refreshment in time of summer heat. Electric light had been established, and there was a singular medley of modern refinement and good and bad taste of the East. The Persian "Tree of Life" was constantly repeated in the wall decorations. I glanced rather carelessly at what I supposed to be the play room of the Amir's children full of toys; great was my amazement to learn afterwards that they were provided for the amusement of his wives!

A new palace for the Czar has been built about half a mile from the station. The sumptuous furniture and decorations are to be sent from Petersburg. I should have thought that it would be more interesting to fill it with specimens of native art.

The fascination of the bazaar leaves no time for historical reflections. We remember afterwards that at Buchara "Iskander" astonished the world with his prowess in the chase of the lion as well as with his success in arms. We forget the innumerable sieges and plunderings through long centuries; but we cannot quite forget the name of *Chingiz Khan*, who rode into a mosque and threw the Koran upon

SHAH ZINDEH, SAMARKAND

the ground before he pillaged the city with his ferocious troops in 1219; nor of Timur the Tartar, equally relentless in war, but a lover of state and splendour, and the arts that could glorify his name. His rule in Buchara has been called the era of its renaissance.

It has been the fashion of late years to select the most odious characters known to us in history and by a process of white-washing to present them to us in a totally different light. Gibbon, I believe, was the first to lead the way in this peculiar idiosyncrasy. His choice fell upon the terrible Mongol, Chingiz Khan; he tells us that "after his first victory, he placed seventy cauldrons on the fire, and seventy of the most guilty rebels were cast headlong into the boiling water. The boldest chieftains might tremble when they beheld, enchased in silver, the skull of the Khan of the Keraites, who, under the name of Prester John, had corresponded with the Roman Pontiff and the princes of Europe. Ninety Chinese cities were stormed or starved by the Mongols, and Zingis, from a knowledge of the filial piety of the Chinese, covered his vanguard with their captive parents. The siege of Pekin was long and laborious; the inhabitants were reduced by famine to decimate and devour their fellow-citizens; when their ammunition was spent, they discharged ingots of gold and silver from their engines; but the Mongols introduced a mine to the centre of the Capital and the conflagration of the palace burnt above thirty days—and five northern provinces were added to the Empire of Zingis. Our European battles, says a philosophic writer (Voltaire), are petty skirmishes if compared to the numbers that have fought and fallen in the fields of Asia. Seven hundred thousand Mongols and Tartars are said to have marched under the standards of Zingis and his four sons, and in the first battle one hundred thousand Carizmians were slain. This was in the war against Mohammed, Sultan of Carizme, who reigned from the Persian Gulf to the borders of India and Turkestan. Zingis besieged and took Otrar, Bokhara, Samarcand, Herat, Merou, Balch, Candahar . . . and ruined a tract of many hundred miles, which was adorned with the habitations and labours of mankind, and five centuries have not been sufficient to repair the ravages of four years. The Mogul Emperor encouraged or indulged the fury of his troops; the hope of future possession was lost in the ardour of rapine and slaughter. . . . Native fierceness was exasperated by a pretence of justice and revenge." After this terrible picture of ravage and destruction Gibbon adds that " Zingis died in the fulness of years and glory, with his last breath exhorting and instructing his sons to achieve the conquest of the Chinese Empire. . . . It is the religion of Zingis that best deserves our wonder and applause. His first and only article of faith was the existence of one GOD, the author of all good. . . . He respected the prophets and pontiffs of the hostile sects —his reason was not informed by books; the

Khan could neither read nor write . . . his harem consisted of five hundred women."

The unhappy and uncertain character of the great historian may account for this singular admiration for a monster of cruelty, but it is really amazing to read the opinion of General Kuropatkin—" Les deux plus grandes figures historiques de l'Asie Centrale, Gengis Khan et Tamerlan, ont eu sur les destinées de la Kashgarie une influence énorme, quoique bien différente. Le premier la conquit sans verser une goutte de sang, y introduisit la tolérence religieuse, encouragea l'industrie, le commerce et les arts, et fonda ainsi la prosperité du pays, qui devint bientôt floressant. Le second, au contraire, y porta le pillage et le massacre, et détruisit en quelque mois, pour longtemps, si ce n'est pour toujours, ce que Gengis Khan et ses descendans avaient mis 170 ans à créer."

I think that with more justice we may look upon the great Tamerlane as a tremendous conqueror, but also as a magnificent sovereign. We read of his receiving a former opponent

TOMB OF TIMUR (EXTERIOR), SAMARKAND

with "all the honour due to a prince, none of the prescribed ceremonies being neglected; he and his retinue were loaded with magnificent presents, such as gold and jewels, robes of honour and girdles, arms, armour, horses, camels, tents, cymbals, chargers, slaves, standards and such like things." The splendid buildings at Samarkand were not the creation of a savage barbarian. We read also that "Amir Timur," as he was called by the Turks and Tartars, was overwhelmed with grief at the loss of his son, and was with difficulty roused to the performance of his duties to his people. "He instituted many pious works, and gave alms to be distributed in the form of food to the poor and indigent." It is true that the records of the gigantic crimes of Chingiz Khan were written by the victims of his conquests, but we do not hear of any traditions that relieve the blackness of his place in history.

The variety of ways of spelling the names of places, of Emperors, Shahs, Amirs and Khans is a difficulty in the study of Eastern nations. For instance, the name of the great Mongol chief has been written Zingis, Gengis, Djinghis, Chingiz, and I know not how many other ways. Gibbon explained that he chose Zingis because "Zin" in the Mongol tongue signifies *great*, and "*gis*" is the superlative termination. "Zingis accepted this appellation of the *most great* after a supposed vision which conferred upon him a divine right to the domain of the earth." In French the name is written Gengis, and this form was adopted in England, for the reason, I suppose, that when an Englishman is in doubt about the pronunciation of a foreign word he invariably utters it as he would if it were French: "ch" in English, is always pronounced "tch." The only exceptions that I can remember are "chaise," "champagne," and a few more words obviously borrowed from across the silver streak. "J" and "g" in English sound generally with the suspicion of a "d" before them, more or less strongly accentuated; therefore we should pronounce in exactly the same way the name of the town on the Oxus whether it were spelt *Charjui* or *Tchardjui*. It is difficult to be consistent in spelling names that are not very well known. Where the French write "ou" we may with the Russians and Germans write "u," provided that we do not say "you," but "oo" as in "food": thus Batum or Batoum, Baku or Bakou, Timur or Timour. The name of the Minister of War is properly spelt Kuropatkin, but he himself in signing his name to foreigners writes it in French "Kouropatkine." "O" in Russian is pronounced "a" unless marked with an accent. English people generally write "Amir" or "Ameer," which is pronounced almost the same as the French "Emir." The name of the founder of Islam used to be written "Mahomet" in English as it is in French. I have adopted the ugly form "Mohammed" in deference to many learned writers; but we are told by students of Eastern languages that "Muhammad" is the correct form, "this being the passive participle of the verb "hamada" signifying "to praise." I have written Buchara not Bokhara, because that spelling more nearly approaches the Russian pronunciation.

Another difficulty in the history of Central Asia and Turkestan is the confusion in the names of countries and races. Ancient writers often speak of a town as if it were a country. The settlements of the nomad tribes were sometimes called by their names, and the designation continued after they had migrated to other places. It was also a common practice over the greater part of Asia for one nation to call another by a reproachful nickname, which was afterwards used by grave historians. Chingiz Khan was of noble birth, his family name was "Temugin." He fought his first battle at the age of thirteen, when he was defeated and forced to fly; at the age of forty he issued from the northern district of Chinese Tartary at the head of his Mongol followers, to overrun the whole of Asia north of India. These wild hordes styled themselves "Turks," but rejected the name of "Tartar."

The name of Tartar or Tatar was, however, applied to the Mongols by their western neighbours, and from them became common in Europe. It was in vogue down to modern times to indicate the nomadic tribes who lived in the steppes or deserts and led a pastoral or unsettled life. But it was not so throughout Central Asia, where the name of Turk was applied to such classes. According to some authorities, the word *Turk* was used in opposition to *Sart*, the real meaning of which is *merchant*; it was a term applied by the nomads (Kirghiz, Kassáks, etc.) to the dwellers in settled habitations whether Turks or Tajiks. The word Sart is little used in the East excepting by Russians. The Mongols, during their ascendancy, gave names of their own to many places, which, after the decline of their power, became obsolete. In the same way, the conquests of Timur seem to have given birth to names that are peculiar to that period alone.

When Chingíz Khan at his death divided

his conquests among his sons, the provinces of Ferghana and Turkestan of modern times fell to Chagatai, and were known collectively as Moghulistan. The Moghul Khans became to all intents and purposes Turks. Moghulistan and Jatah were one and the same country. The Chagatais called the Moghuls "Jatah" by way of depreciation. It had no racial signification, but meant "a ne'er-do-well" or "rascal." The Moghuls called the Chagatais "Karavenas." This region formerly belonged to the Uighurs, a name which means "five cities." The land of the "six cities" is a different region, in the central desert with its moving sands and buried towns.

With the introduction of the Musulman religion, tribes lost their characteristics. The religious feeling of the people of East Turkestan is stronger than in any part of Central Asia; but they are cowards as well as fanatics, the result perhaps of tyranny and persecution. In the region of the Six Cities we find the centre of fanaticism. The inhabitants keep themselves apart from other tribes; they are Chinese in appearance, but sober and industrious. Blue is never worn by these zealous Musulmans, because the colour is a favourite with *unbelievers*. These people were late in accepting the Koran, but, like the Albanians in European Turkey, they became more zealous and intolerant than their instructors. Chiefs of tribes changed their ideas and customs more rapidly than their people on account of intermarriages, it being usual when one Khan subdued another, to demand a sister or daughter in marriage; and great personages often added foreign wives to their harems.

It was the desire of all the tribes and nations of Central Asia to identify themselves with the race which happened to be in the ascendant at any particular time. They endeavoured to adopt its name and to pass themselves off as members of the nation in supremacy, regardless of racial affinities.

The sons and grandsons of Chingiz Khan were slow to give up their wandering lives, living in tents when not pursuing their conquests. The sign of a change was when they came to dwell in a house. Chagatai would have forfeited the allegiance of his subjects had he done so, and therefore he never settled in the towns of Buchara or Samarkand. The country between these towns is the most fertile portion of Central Asia ; it is watered by the Zarafshan (*the gold dispenser*), so called from the wonderful richness of the soil in the country through which it passes. It has been used for the purposes of irrigation from the earliest ages. Many of these details I have taken from the " Tarikh-I-Rashidi."

The town of Samarkand is about six miles from the railway station. The roads are planted on both sides with parallel rows of poplars, in some places as many as eight or ten rows ; this gives you the impression of entering an immense park. The effect is, however, spoilt by the terrible dust and the extraordinary width of the roads. There are some good modern shops in this Russian

TOMB OF TIMUR (INTERIOR), SAMARKAND

quarter. The best silks and china come from Tashkend. The silk fabrics are similar to those of China or Japan, but still finer, with a peculiar brightness or sheen upon them. As at Buchara, there is much delicate silver work in the style of the Trichinopoli filigree. The buildings are all of one storey on account of the frequent occurrence of earthquakes.

The parks are very extensive, and well laid out. Near the principal Russian church a very interesting museum is being arranged, and will no doubt eventually be of great use to students in Central Asia. There was here a heap of stones and clay roughly broken, brought from an ancient city, now completely destroyed, and on some pieces I saw rudely carved the Cross, which indicates that the building must have existed in Christian times. Among snakes and other unpleasant creatures preserved in bottles, was a small monster, something like a scorpion, which has hitherto been known to exist only in one part of America. The finest specimens of all descriptions of ancient art that are found are sent to the Hermitage at Petersburg. A visit to a well-managed orphanage showed that the care of the poor and friendless is not neglected at Samarkand. As usual there was an *icon*—a sacred picture—in every room. With feelings akin to impatience I gave my attention to objects of interest that seemed to delay the arrival at the point of *supreme* interest.

From the moment that you arrive at Samarkand your mind is filled with recollections of the great Timur Lenk—the lame—to the exclusion of all other subjects. Your first thought is to visit his tomb and city. This is the goal that has been looked forward to throughout the long journey—roughly speaking, about four thousand five hundred miles.

My personal interest in the great conqueror dates from nursery days, when on a little toy theatre I found the drama of "Timour the Tartar" of thrilling interest. I visited the mausoleum alone, and felt a singular dreamlike sensation standing by the tomb of the terrible hero, under the great dome, with a

TOMB OF TIMUR, TRACING OF DESIGN ON JADE

Musulman as my sole companion. The spot is certainly awe-inspiring. I was not aware at the time that there was any real danger in the situation, and my silent friend gravely helped me to hold my tracing paper, as I made a rubbing of the beautiful carving on the upper sides of the dark, black-green slab of jade, the largest in the world, which covers the stone exactly over the grave, which is in the crypt below. In the design I found the Cross, which I feel certain is a proof that the jade had been formerly used in some Christian building. On other parts of the slab are carved lines from the Koran. The "ja" or jade stone is highly prized, and in former times was believed to be found in no other part of the world. Near to the tomb of Tamerlane, at his feet is that of his tutor, and close by lie two of his sons. A white marble balustrade encloses these memorials, and I was able to obtain a rubbing of its exquisitely carved ornamentation, the design of which leaves no doubt that this must once have been the sanctuary railing of a Christian church. On the ground also I noticed the Cross upon several broken slabs. In almost every design it is possible to discern a cross, but not as it is to be seen here. In the fourteenth and fifteenth centuries there were still many Christians at Samarkand, and the Musulman architects and sculptors who worked for the glorification of Tamerlane must have been perfectly aware of the meaning of the Christian symbol, and would certainly not have chosen it for the adornment of a mosque. They, however, would not have hesitated to make use of any beautiful work of art taken from a Christian church, any more than to adapt the whole of a church to their form of worship. I could not obtain any information on the subject, and it did not appear to excite any interest when I mentioned it. The mosaic enamels outside the building are very fine, and the wonderful turquoise dome and lofty leaning tower form a group of most impressive grandeur. The spot is lonely, and inspires solemn thoughts of the instability of

TOMB OF TIMUR (EXTERIOR), SAMARKAND

mere human glory. Europe, as well as Asia, trembled at the name of this great man. His name will for ever be memorable in history; and yet, in little more than four centuries after his death, the splendid mausoleum erected in his honour is crumbling away, and in this nineteenth century a solitary traveller will feel his spirit daunted by the gloom that is inseparable from all that speaks of change and decay. I could have lingered within the enclosure forgetful of time but for the exasperating interruption of noisy children begging and crowding round me, so that I was obliged to retreat in haste to my drosky and indicate to the driver, with many signs and disconnected Russian words, the road I wished to take in order to visit the mosques and tombs of the family of Tamerlane.

The road leads through a dreary outskirt of the town, beside an immense burial-ground, clay-coloured and dusty and unspeakably depressing, spreading away as far as the eye can reach until the horizon is bounded by lovely snow-capped mountains. On each side of the road I saw the unhappy lepers who are allowed to sit here begging; they do not attempt to approach, but hold out bowls to catch the alms thrown to them.

On entering the Shah Zindeh you see before you a steep ascent of many steps, with, on both sides, beautiful doorways to the sepulchres of the family of the great Timur. A street of tombs, some of them extremely simple, others richly decorated with Persian enamels. The colouring is chiefly turquoise blue and indigo, with flowing lines of cream colour and brown, all in the perfect harmony that is not produced in modern days. Some of the mosques at Constantinople have similar tiles of a rather later date, but where restoration's defacing fingers have passed the pale delicate blues and pearly greys have stiffened into sharp outlines and crude bright hues.

The oft-disputed question of restoration or no restoration is here constantly forced upon the attention. It is melancholy to see these

SHAH ZINDEH, SAMARKAND

exquisite works of art gradually falling into decay ; but, as it would be impossible to reproduce them in the beauty of their first colouring, it is perhaps better to leave unspoiled what still remains as a school of art for future generations. There is no danger of destruction by the ruthless hands of tourists, and the Russians are beginning to awake to a sense of the dignity of art and of antiquity.

The centre of interest in these buildings is the sacred mosque built by Tamerlane over the tomb of Kussan, a cousin of the prophet. I entered, accompanied by two Mollahs, through a beautiful doorway. The door itself is wonderful in carving and inlaid workmanship. The light within is dim, and the spot is held in such veneration by the Musulmans that silence is enjoined, and the places of special interest are indicated without speech. The tomb of Kussan is imperfectly seen through a grating, it is covered with the folds of fine cashmire that are customary, and the green flag and horse's tail, with other relics, are held in the most profound respect. A very large and valuable copy of the Koràn is also shown. Stepping lightly and glancing with admiration at all these treasures, I turned to leave the mosque and suddenly observed that the outer door had been shut, and that three or four silent Mollahs had made their appearance. A feeling of uneasiness came over me—was the rumour true that I had heard of women not being allowed to enter mosques, that the presence of strangers everywhere was unwelcome, and that they owed their safety to the strict orders of the Russian general that they were not to be molested? I bowed my thanks generally for the courtesy shown me and moved, not too hurriedly, to the point of egress. Great was my relief when the wonderful door was suddenly thrown open, and exactly in front of me was an English gentleman, Kodak in hand. There was laughter on both sides, but for once, I am afraid, the snapshot was not a success. The grave Mollahs smiled, waited patiently while I endeavoured

SACRED TOMB, SHAH ZINDEH

to make sketches of some lovely patterns in tiles, and finally offered me sweetmeats, accompanying me down the steep steps to the road where my carriage was waiting.

The roads at Samarkand are fairly good. In the park they are perfect for cycling, and must be highly appreciated. The weather was all that could be desired, warm and dry, although it was already December. The nights were frosty but marvellously beautiful; not in the least like the dazzling brightness that we see in Italy, but softly gleaming with a strange stillness that sent one's thoughts wandering back to the shepherds that watched their flocks on a certain night that brought hope and comfort to every being on earth.

The medressé and mosque of the Chinese Princess Bibi, wife of Tamerlane, is one of the grandest monuments in Samarkand. An earthquake in September 1897 rent the building with a gaping fissure, and the recurrence of such an accident will probably complete its destruction. Bibi Khanym was said to be the favourite wife of the Tartar prince. The huge marble lectern, or resting-place for the Koràn, opposite to the entrance of the building, is the only thing that shows no sign of ruin.

The great Righistan, or market place, is the centre of life in Samarkand. On three sides of the square are gigantic medressés—one built by Ulugh Beg, the grandson of Timur, 1421, is the oldest; that called Shir Dar, from the lion in enamel tiles which is on the façade, was built in 1601; and the third, called Tillah Kari from its gold decoration of which there is now no trace, dates from 1618. Lord Curzon considered the Righistan of Samarkand to be "the noblest public square in the world." I have never seen any place with which it can be compared. From the top of the Shir Dar (*frontispiece*)—a formidable climb—you look down, without a parapet of any description, upon the busy crowd of men dwarfed to the size of ants. It is a relief to forget the giddy prospect and gaze upon the lovely mountains that know no change, and must always enchant

MOSQUE OF BIBI KHANYM, SAMARKAND

the eyes that behold them. English eyes gaze with a special interest, feeling that not very far off on the other side we should meet with the advance guard of our own countrymen. These thoughts naturally find no utterance in the presence of Russian friends.

I wandered about alone in the Righistan for a long time, unmolested and almost unnoticed, wishing to impress the scene upon my mind. As a question of true art, I cannot think it consistent that buildings of stupendous dimensions should be decorated outside with fragile and delicate ornamentation, but this is the general rule in the East, and the same remark may be applied to the beautiful Duomo at Florence. I was surprised to observe the dog tooth moulding in huge proportions at the foot of the minarets, each of which diverges more or less from the perpendicular. It was extremely amusing to observe the ways of the people, the strange mixture of business and pleasure. I drew near to a group of men, in sitting position, surrounding an old and prosperous looking individual also seated cross-legged, who appeared to be preaching to them; at last it dawned upon me that he was telling stories that were listened to with the greatest interest, and his air of self-satisfaction when he paused for a moment to refresh himself with sherbet, or some beverage of the kind, was inimitable.

The bazaar is uninteresting, and has in a great measure lost its Oriental colouring. I visited silk and plush manufactories with antiquated hand-looms, but the harsh and sticky colours spoke in some cases unmistakably of aniline dyes. An Englishman living in Samarkand for business purposes greeted his countrymen with pleasure, not having heard his own language for more than two years.

The name of Tamerlane is so indissolubly connected with Samarkand that one is apt to forget the vicissitudes of the last four centuries. Here in his wonderful capital we can dwell upon the magnificence of his court, forgetful of the terrible massacres and the destruction of life and property for which he was respon-

MOSQUE OF ULUGH BEG, RIGHISTAN, SAMARKAND

sible. The conquests of Timur from Delhi to the near neighbourhood of Moscow are recorded in some of Gibbon's most eloquent pages. He rejoices over the capture of the Sultan Bajazet at the celebrated battle of Angora, the site of the victory of Pompey over Mithridates, B.C. 66. Timur accepted in early life the Moslem faith, according to the belief of the Shiahs, and excused some of his enormous cruelties with the pretext of revenge for the death of Ali and his son Hossein. It was his custom after victory to view the piles of heads of the vanquished, hideously arranged in columns and pyramids. We are reminded of the heads of the seventy sons of Ahab. The numbers of his victims, given by Oriental historians, are probably immensely exaggerated, and are mere figures of speech.

The wonderful railway which is now completed to Andijan, the capital of Ferghana, passes soon after leaving Samarkand by the celebrated "Iron Gate," spoken of in connection with Timur because of his frequent passages across the Zarafshan, but the gates which were a reality in ancient times had disappeared long before his era. They are mentioned by a Chinese writer, A.D. 630, as closing the defile and being clamped with iron. The pass was known as the Kalugha, a name often given to narrow gorges; among the best known is the Kalugha in the wall of Alexander, near Derbent, on the Caspian Sea.

The completion of the Transcaspian line brings the Russians into direct communication with the country north of the Hindu Kush, by means of the good military roads which they have already made over some of the passes of the Pamir country. It seems ungracious to find fault with the rulers of a nation by whom you have been kindly received, but General Kuropatkin has himself spoken harshly of the English, not, we are willing to believe, from feelings of personal dislike, but as the expression of his opinion of our character and policy. He has permitted the translator of his book on the Anglo-Russian Frontier to

DECORATIVE WORK, SHAH ZINDEH

make use of the most intemperate and threatening language. After remarking that the British lion dreams of no further conquests in India, but wishes to be left in peace to enjoy the possessions annexed or absorbed, he adds that Russia is continually overflowing her borders from the frozen steppes of the North. "Chaque jour un pas en avant la rapproche des pays du soleil qu'elle convoite et veut arracher à l'Angleterre. Déjà les deux rivales n'ont plus entre elles, sur quelques points, qu'une bande de territoire assez étroite . . . la lutte doit inévitablement éclater entre elles. On comprend par suite avec quel soin chacune étudie ce futur champ de bataille. La Russie surtout, obligée de prendre l'offensive, ne cesse d'y envoyer ses éclaireurs. Des missions politiques, scientifiques, géographiques ou militaires parcourent sans relâche, dans tous les sens, ces pays dont les noms barbares sont à peine connus chez nous. Les diplomates et les généraux russes en étudient l'histoire présente et passée ; ils évaluent soigneusement les ressources qu'ils possèdent et les revenues qu'on en peut tirer. . . . Le but de ces travaux n'est douteux pour personne et l'on n'en fait pas mystère. Les soldats du tsar préparent dès aujourd'hui la conquête de la Kachgarie et viendront probablement s'y heurter bientôt à ceux de l'impératrice des Indes. Quel que soit le résultat du choc, il sera rude et le contre-coup s'en fera sentir au loin."

This is plain speaking and cannot be considered as merely an expression of private opinion.

It is strange that English writers upon Russia are either violently hostile or else see all that concerns that empire through rose-coloured spectacles. We know Russia to be the most thinly populated country in Europe, and yet Mr Jefferson, in his book "Roughing it in Siberia," says "the Russian government seems to be making an honest effort to relieve the congestion of some of its European provinces by encouraging a great emigration to Siberia." Mr Jefferson thinks that this was at least one of the main objects in constructing the Siberian railway. Russia has always practised the removal of large masses of people from one country to another. We heard lately that a peace-loving sect, holding some of the opinions of Quakers, was to be transported to the island of Cyprus, it has now taken refuge in Canada, while the return to Russian territory of the miserable Armenian refugees is demanded from Turkey.

In the interesting life of Mr Roebuck lately published, we are given part of one of his speeches in the last year of his life, 1878, in which he said that his duty to England and the interests of his country had guided him through life. "I have not sought in party politics my line of conduct, but I have looked forward and asked myself this question—Does this conduce to the honour and happiness of England? England has been the sun by which I have guided my course. When I follow the interests of England, I follow the interests of the whole human race." The action of Russia in Turkey, ostensibly for the deliverance of the Christians, he treated with scorn, exclaiming—" The poor Christian! I want to know how Russia treated the poor Catholic! Was the Catholic not a Christian in her mind? She whipped the Catholic into the Greek Church and that she called Christianity! The war with Turkey, in my mind, is a thoroughly unjust proceeding on the part of Russia; she is no less barbarous than Turkey; she is far more dishonest. I have no admiration for the Turkish government, but I do not believe that the substitution of Russia for Turkey would be a benefit to the wretched people who are made the pretext for the present invasion."

Roebuck spoke as an ardent patriot, but his love of his country did not inspire him with stronger expressions than have been used by Professor Vambéry who wrote: " With the British flag appears the dawn of a better era in every zone and in every quarter of the world."

It would have been interesting to learn something of the life of women in Central Asia, but "any violation, by word or deed, of the secrecy of the harem is an unpardonable offence among the Turkish nations." Miss Sykes, in her interesting book about Persia, expresses the same feeling and says that it was "contrary to all laws of Eastern etiquette to question them on their womankind, in whom I was deeply interested."

My questions upon all subjects were cut short by a severe attack of influenza, which made the return journey almost entirely a blank to me. The kind attention of the Russian gentlemen who superintended the expedition procured for me the help of three medical men at different stations on the line; but I was unable to leave the *travelling hotel* until the change to the boat at Krasnovodsk.

The weather during the whole journey was simply perfect. Buchara, in the same latitude as Rome and New York, does not think of reminding you in December that summer is over.

One painful reminiscence of this wonderful journey was the sight of a group of prisoners bound for Siberia, among them one woman. They were chained to prevent escape, but there appeared to be no unnecessary severity. I was allowed, with an English gentleman, to offer the means of procuring for them some small comforts to cheer them in their terrible fate.

The dreary desert appeared to me unspeakably dreary, dotted at intervals with the watch towers that speak of the cruel days of slave-hunting. The only vegetation was the *camel thorn*, the food of those long-suffering animals, that is used to keep together the dangerous sands to which palisades of wood offer but feeble resistance. Moslem armies in these terrible deserts were allowed to perform the prescribed ablutions with sand instead of water.

At Askabad I was unable to accept the invitations kindly offered to the English travellers, but I was not without compensation in a different line. Before leaving England I pro-

CAMELS IN THE DESERT

vided myself with Russian cigarettes, having heard that it was customary for ladies to smoke on all occasions. I carefully smoked one to be sure that I should suffer no ill effects; but I forgot all about them until, at Askabad, a train full of young Polish recruits drew up in line with my home or hospital. The happy thought occurred to me to hand out from the corridor to the opposite window the elegant little case of useless luxuries. The success of the idea was so great that an English gentleman procured for me at the station a supply of cigarettes sufficient for the whole train; they may not have been of superior quality, but they gave pleasure.

A short delay at Khizil Arvat attracted the inhabitants to the station, and I was painfully impressed with their appearance of squalid misery. The women especially had a look of hopeless degradation. Some of the men were amused at my showers of chocolates upon the children and helped to pick them up.

A second visit to Baku does but deepen

one's feelings of disgust, but the lovely country from Tiflis to Batum is equally charming by day or by night. The beauty of the Crimean littoral centering in Yalta and Livadia is too well known to require any description.

Lovely Yalta! My first view of it was just before daybreak, when, driven to despair by the noise of the windlass landing and taking in merchandise, I made a hasty toilette and hurried up on deck. A cold greyness was over everything, the snow on the mountains shone like steel; by degrees 1 became aware of a pinky light on the more distant ranges. It seemed to be too soon for sunrise, but, as I stood gazing, the glow deepened in strange contrast with the intense blue-whiteness of the nearer peaks, and gradually, as night gave way to dawn, the soft beauty of the enchanting spot was revealed.

Frolicsome dolphins sported around, whisking their tails in the air; heavy blundering porpoises were scarcely less indifferent to our curious inspection. But no time was to be lost, and I was anxious to make the most of the short delay before starting for Sevastopol. Catching sight of a church picturesquely situated on an eminence, I hurried off in that direction and obtained a charming view of the little town and closely encircling mountains. A devout crowd of worshippers filled the building in honour of the birthday of the Czar, and many, unable to obtain admission, joined in the service from outside. For once, *short cuts* answered their purpose, and I was able to hurry along the pretty promenade and obtain a general idea of the gay and picturesque little town. A piercing whistle from the steamer recalled me to a prosaic view of things, and I ran back with all possible speed to be in time for the moment of departure.

The most prosaic mind cannot resist daydreams in an atmosphere so full of legend, and history which is half legend. Dreams of Jason and the Golden Fleece, dreams of Iphigenia, of Prometheus; memories of the great Mithridates, of Genoese and Venetian pride, of the ravages of Mongols and Tartars, and sad memories of our gallant countrymen whose lives were heroically given for their Queen and country in the long Crimean War.

These last memories crowd upon one's mind on entering the splendid harbour of Sevastopol. We are told that it will soon become the great Russian arsenal on the Black Sea, closed for commerce and for ordinary travellers. We will not dwell upon this disregard of treaties, but let our last thoughts be those of peace and goodwill. If statesmen and newspaper writers would refrain from stirring up feelings of enmity, England and Russia might work together for the good of mankind. Earnestly hoping that this happy solution of difficulties may be accomplished, I close this short account of a marvellously interesting journey.

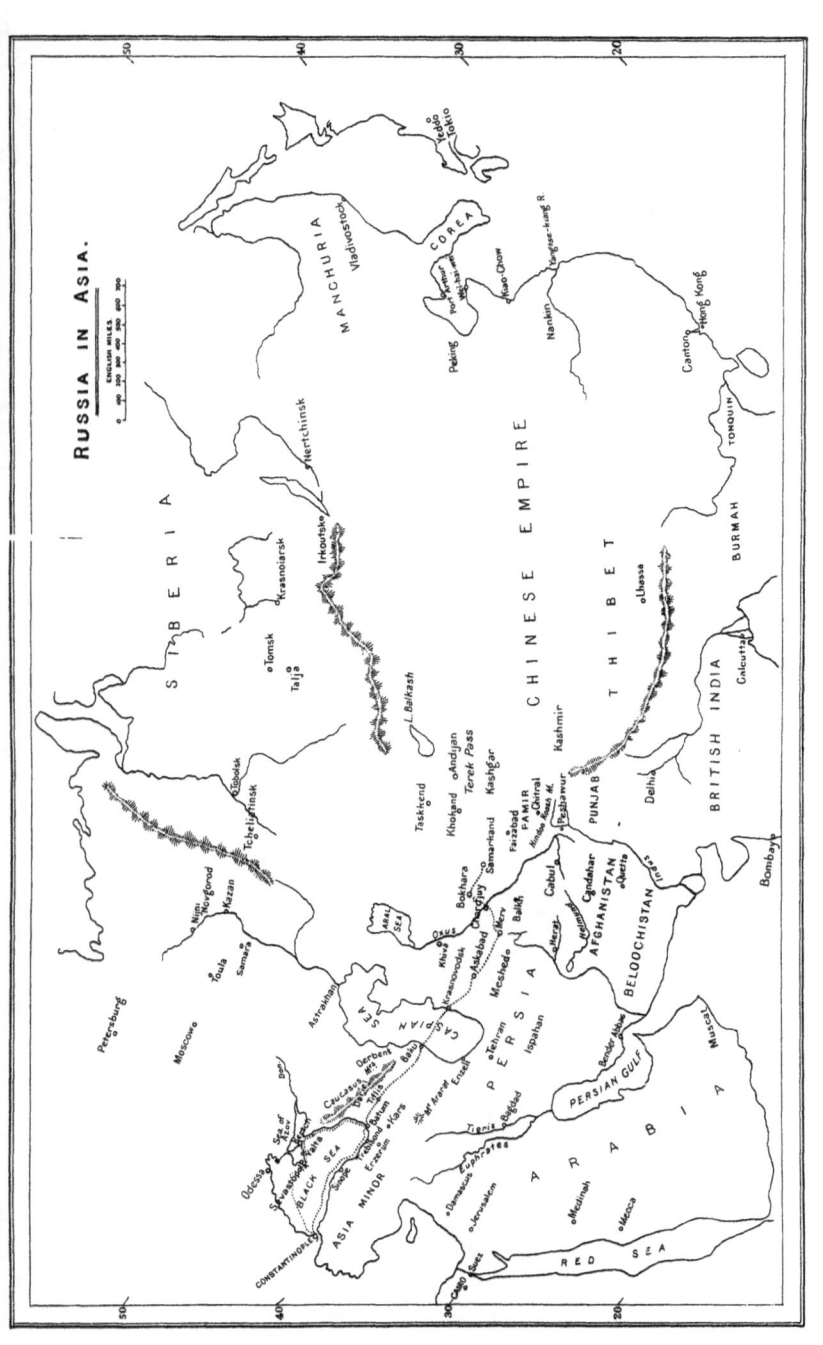

PRINTED BY
TURNBULL AND SPEARS,
EDINBURGH

www.ingramcontent.com/pod-product-compliance
Lightning Source LLC
Chambersburg PA
CBHW020648230426
43665CB00008B/352